HAND SPINNING

ESSENTIAL TECHNICAL AND CREATIVE SKILLS

HAND SPINNING

ESSENTIAL TECHNICAL
AND CREATIVE SKILLS

PAM AUSTIN

THE CROWOOD PRESS

First published in 2018 by
The Crowood Press Ltd
Ramsbury, Marlborough
Wiltshire SN8 2HR

enquiries@crowood.com
www.crowood.com

This impression 2021
© Pam Austin 2018

British Library Cataloguing-in-Publication Data
A catalogue record for this book is available from the British Library.

ISBN 978 1 78500 373 8

Graphic design and layout by Peggy & Co. Design
Printed and bound in India by Parksons Graphics

Contents

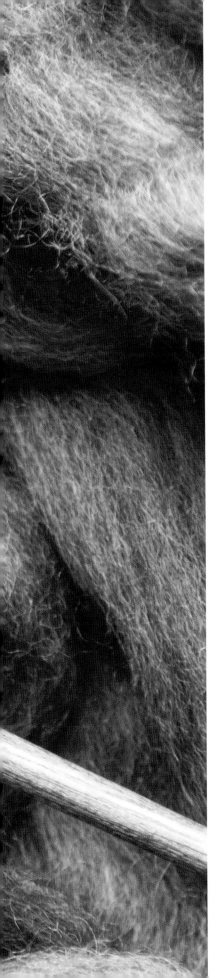

Acknowledgements

To my family and late husband who deserve medals for their love, support and tolerance of my lifelong 'wooliness'. The book would be of little value, and far less interest, without the inspired photography of Dorte Kjaerulff and watercolour illustrations by Jane Heynes. I am extremely grateful for their gifted work, and particularly for the enthusiasm and patience with which they delivered it.

To my daughter Jenny, and friends Gillian Petrie and Frances Cubbon for their personal assistance, mentoring and practical contributions.

To current pupils Erica, Frances, Jane, Mary, Rosalind and Val, whose accomplished work is credited where it appears.

To my teacher Elizabeth Palmer, whose unsurpassed standards have stood me in good stead for thirty years and more. And last, but not least, a thank you to my many, many pupils past and present for the sheer pleasure they have given me and, not least, for their generosity in helping me learn so much!

Pam Austin

Introduction

Before I introduce you to the skills and ultimate joys of the world of wool, I want to give you a small insight into the path that has taken me to this privileged position of fulfilment in my craft. This might help you to understand me as a person as I speak to you through this book.

I am a woman of a certain age now, but let me take you back to the mid-1980s. My personal life was crumbling before my eyes with a failing marriage, no money and three children who needed me. Rather rashly, I spent my £12 weekly housekeeping on Jaeger yarn and some knitting needles. I knew of a spinning school based in a property where a beloved aunt used to live. I had spent happy times there as a child in her barn watching chicks hatch and stirring the boiling pig potatoes. It was a centre of positivity and happiness. So, of course, it was meant to be that I should learn to spin in that same spot. The rest is history and determination.

SPINNING IS FOR PLEASURE!

The purpose of this book is to enlighten, encourage and inspire spinners to learn new skills, and become competent, discerning and creative spinners, whose work brings lasting pleasure. There are so many ways to spin; a world of fibre and ways of preparing it. There is a whole spectrum of colour to work with and there are dozens of different yarn structures to choose from. Avoid the treadmill of 2-ply and aspire to spin yarn that is as exquisite and unique as the hands that spin it.

No-one has written the rule book on spinning. There are as many opinions about every aspect of spinning as there are stars in the sky; the range of handspun yarn is infinite too.

A comprehensive knowledge of spinning techniques, fibres, yarn structure and colour skills will instill the confidence needed to try something new. Hopefully it will inspire unique and beautiful yarn that has mindfulness and meaning – and experience the enormous pleasure this brings.

The feeling of being 'not very creative, or good with colour' soon disappears when you know where to find inspiration and how to work with colour.

People are fascinated to watch a spinner take a raw fleece and turn it into yarn. It looks relaxing and peaceful. Using your senses to pick out the perfect fleece for hand spinning saves time and frustration.

Spinning is steady, rhythmic and mindful – and a satisfying way to enjoy what nature provides. It is a great use of natural resources, too: a low cost, environmentally friendly way to relax and enjoy leisure time. The UK Campaign for Wool is raising awareness of the valuable properties of wool and the result of this fascinating craft is a plethora of 'woolly' things to use, wear and offer as gifts.

There is much to learn; fortunately, you do not have to learn it all at once. After getting started with a drop spindle or simple wheel, the later chapters in this book can be worked through, or dipped into in any order as needed.

The purpose of the spinning wheel is actually quite simple: to make twist and store yarn on a bobbin. All the would-be spinner needs to do is learn how to put fibre and twist together and the yarn is made. Learn this one trick, and a lifetime of creativity and pleasure is in store for you. All learning requires a bit of effort, and like any dynamic activity – riding a bicycle, driving a car or swimming – if you stop, it falls apart! But spinning is not dangerous: you won't drown if it goes wrong, nor is it particularly difficult.

A traditional spinning wheel has its own mystique. Watch the wheel turning, twist flowing along the fibre, bobbin spinning round and then, apparently, stopping still. It is mesmerizing to watch such a timeless skill: a fascinating mix of activity that somehow manages to look both busy and calm simultaneously.

With helpful instruction it should not take you long to spin your first skein. The sheer joy of holding your own first hand-spun yarn is totally out of proportion to the use most spinners make of it! It is fair to say that first spinning is usually 'variable', to find the kindest word, but it has its own unique value. It is the benchmark against which future work will be compared.

Start a record book and keep a sample for comparison and a measure of progress. Good pupils, like good teachers, never stop learning. There is no need to adopt unrealistic standards of consistency or accept rigorous judgmental standards. Spinners own their spinning and spin for their own pleasure and purpose. There is no right or wrong way to spin, nor is there a way of 'doing it properly'. The correct way is the way that feels right for you.

You spin. You rule how it is done. And the more knowledge you have of the subject, the more satisfying spinning will be.

There are recognized spinning techniques which have been used for hundreds of years, such as 'long draw' and 'worsted draw', which serve different purposes. However, a good yarn is one that is fit for purpose, and a good spinner has the knowledge, skills and discernment to choose a manner of spinning which fits their purpose.

The pleasure of drawing out an arm's-length of thread, seeing the lumps and bumps smooth out as the fibres attenuate, never ceases. Equally satisfying is combing out a fine Shetland fleece in the traditional manner.

Spinning is for pleasure and one of its many joys is spinning yarn that money can't buy or be produced or replicated on a commercial scale. The purpose of a yarn need not be practical, such as to weave, knit or crochet into something else; the end purpose may be simply to make beautiful yarn, just for the joy of it. Many spinners make yarn simply for the purpose of art. All art is a personal, subjective response to something and, in this respect, the spinner of art yarn is no different from a watercolour artist. Art yarn is a spinner's response to fibre, texture, colour structure, and so on; therefore it cannot be judged to be right, wrong or 'spun properly'.

A good quality yarn is one that suits the purpose of the spinner. Hence, even those new to spinning can quickly be spinning quality yarn. Learning is a process, so don't make impossible demands; simply choose the purpose to suit ability. Far better to make a hot water bottle cover that gives years of service as your first spinning project, than start a lace-weight shawl with complex detail that never gets finished.

Discovering fibre is an adventure rather like travelling the Old Silk route. A world-wide abundance of quality fleece can be sourced, from primitive to modern cross-breeds, camelid, goat and rabbit fibres. There are traditional plant fibres too, such as flax and cotton, and exotic types like bamboo and banana, and of course silk.

Fibre is only one part of the equation of a yarn, however. Colour is as significant as fibre and the more you work with it, the more fun it becomes. Colour skills are an integral part of creating beautiful yarn. The architectural structure of yarn affects the way it reflects or refracts light, and its texture and performance, so you need to know about that too. Just as cookery has its classic sauces, you will find there are great classic yarns, like glorious shaped bouclé, gimps, crêpe and coils – these are not at all difficult, once you have the recipe.

The rewards of learning to spin are uplifting and wholesome. It takes effort, as any spinner will tell you. Like your first day at a new school, be brave, turn the page, and just get on with it.

You won't be the first....

IN HER HANDS SHE HOLDS THE DISTAFF,
AND GRASPS THE SPINDLE WITH HER FINGERS.

PROVERBS 31:19

1 One Thread at a Time
Getting started on a spindle, or wheel

The aim of this chapter is to show how to spin a simple woollen thread, by hand, with a drop spindle, or by spinning on a wheel. Spinning with a drop spindle was commonplace in all societies for thousands of years and is still the cheapest, easiest and most accessible way to get started. Aim to make a single thread, not commercial-looking yarn; that is not what hand spinning is about. Just let one thread lead to another, and avoid being judgemental.

Spindle whorls, round weights with a hole through which a stick was inserted, are common artefacts in museums. Images of spinners working with drop spindles (whorl on a stick), great wheels or charkhas can be found on ancient pottery fragments, stone carvings and illuminated manuscripts. Textiles rarely survive over the centuries but there are exceptions, such as the Peruvian Paracas textile fragments in the British Museum, which are over 2,000 years old and spun from camel or alpaca. From Europe we have the shroud of St Paulinus of Trier dating from the fourth century. Such textiles show levels of spinning and weaving expertise which are astonishing given what we know of the technology available at the time.

All of the images of spinners show them doing the same thing: mixing fibre and twist and drawing them out into a thread; this has not changed in 2,000 years. Spinning may look mysterious, whether it is done by hand or in a busy commercial mill, but it is simply a process of putting fibre and twist together.

MAKING THREAD WITHOUT A WHEEL OR SPINDLE

This little exercise shows how simple it is to draw a long thread from a few fibres. It demonstrates the relationship between fibre and twist. It assumes availability of a few locks of wool, either straight from the sheep or commercially produced roving (a length of fibres loosely drawn out into a tube or sausage shape) – it does not matter which at this stage.

A wheel or spindle simply *makes* the twist, it doesn't control anything – unless you let it – so for the moment just work with your hands. A woollen thread made by hand can be drawn out to up to a yard or a metre at a time. It is surprising how few fibres it takes to make an arm's-length of yarn.

Children find the following step-by-step exercise easy to follow and love to see their handiwork spring into life as a wristband when the thread is folded in half and naturally twists into a yarn.

There is an inverse relationship between fibre and twist: thin thread needs lots of twist; thick thread needs a lot less – much less in fact. So as thread is drawn out and gets thinner, more twist needs to be put in to strengthen it. At this point you will understand why spindles were invented. Fingers get tired.

STEP 1   Gently tease off a few fibres.

STEP 2   Take a lock of fibre and hold it between finger and thumb of both hands so that the tips of the fibre are pointing up or down and loose fibres hang suspended vertically between thumb and forefinger of both hands. Keep hands close together, but leave fibres free to take up the twist.

STEP 3   With one hand, put in some twist by turning the fibres of one hand over and over, and keep the other hand still. If you let go the twist will escape, so keep hold all the time. Try not to move the hands apart. It will look a complete mess but don't worry about that.

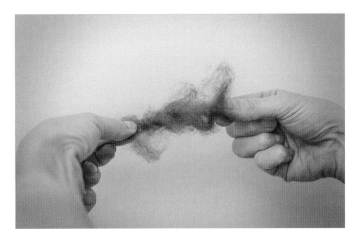

STEP 4 After two or three twists the twist will gather into one place and form a narrow neck. Now gently draw your hands apart and, as if by magic, it won't break. Stop when your hands are about 8 inches apart; put in more twist to form your first hand-spun thread. It's a great feeling! The longer the thread gets, the more twist you will need to put in. Be content with a fat thread at first as this will be less likely to break, and will need much less twist.

STEP 5 Without taking your hands off, put in lots more twist in the same direction and gently draw your hands even further apart. With luck you will feel it stretch as the fibres attenuate and the twist evens itself out along the thread. This feeling of stretchiness is rather like plasticity – the fibre stretches – but unlike elastic it does not shrink back.

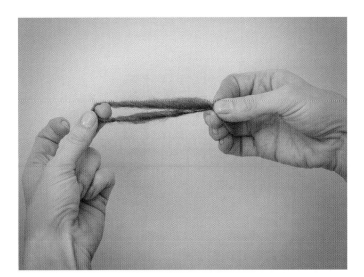

STEP 6 Put in more twist until it feels strong and secure and will not stretch further. Now bring both ends together, keeping a finger in-between. Hold the ends and let go with the finger. The thread will quickly twist back on itself and form double, stable yarn. (This is actually 'plying', but more on that later.)

STEP 7 This can be tied to make a wristband or keyring as a keepsake. If it didn't work first time, try again, paying careful attention to how you hold the fibres. Try to find the very satisfying, stretchy feeling as the fibres slip over each other; this feeling is what you will be looking for when spinning on a wheel or spindle in future.

SPINNING ON A DROP SPINDLE

When you can make a simple thread by hand, the next stage is to get a spindle to make the twist for you. The method is exactly the same as above without a spindle: put twist into fibre, draw thread, add twist and draw. But a lot faster and more satisfying. Spindles come in all shapes and sizes but the easiest by far is the top whorl. This has a whorl at the top with a hook in it and a long spindle stem. A light-weight spindle, say less than an ounce or 30g is best to start with. You simply use it to do what your left hand did in the exercise above – make the twist. It is very important to hold the spindle in your left hand and turn it up towards your body, over and away from you.

When you think about it, spinning is only joining fibres together. If you can join a few fibres to a thread you can spin... so it makes sense to look very closely at how to join fibres to a ready-made thread. Attention to detail in how to make good strong joins is the secret of success.

The following step-by-step exercise demonstrates joining fibre to the previously made thread, which is what spinning is essentially all about: one thread leading to another.

You could use some ready-made yarn as your leader thread, but you would miss the learning opportunity of seeing fibre and twist come together in a carefully controlled manner. Once you have a leader thread attached to the hook than all you need to know is how to join new fibres to a leader thread. With luck, you will soon be spinning.

STEP 1   Firstly, take the spindle in your left hand and hook it into few of the fibres. It is easier to lay the spindle down on a table at first. Leave most of the fibres loose and hold a few at the outer edge of them between finger and thumb as before.

STEP 2   Now gently twirl the spindle up towards you and then away from you. This will put twist into the fibres, forming a neck where the twist has congregated.

STEP 3   When you see the neck has formed, draw out your thread as in stages 4–6 above.

STEP 4   As the thread becomes stronger it will support the weight of the spindle and can be twirled freely in the same direction as before. Once you have about 18 inches of strong thread, fold in half to make a stable yarn.

STEP 5   Unhook the thread and tie it securely onto the spindle stem to make a leader thread.

STEP 6   When the leader thread is attached to the stem with a clove hitch it will not slip.

STEP 7   Use a half-hitch to secure the leader thread to the hook.

MAKING JOINS

Admittedly the method shown is still rather slow, but it allows you time to think about what is going on and what needs to be done, and to do it. Have faith: after two or three goes the spindle will soon be spinning suspended in mid-air. For a start be pleased that you can manage fibre and twist, and make a thread that holds together. This is the most important thing a spinner needs to learn – as stated previously, the very essence of spinning is simply bringing fibre and twist together.

The next stage is to combine the stilted drop spindle movements into one cohesive flowing movement. While the spindle spins in mid-air, both hands are free to draft the thread.

MAKING JOINS

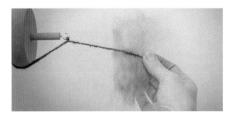

STEP 1   Hold the leader thread across a few fibres half-way down the staple. Lay the thread well over the fibres to ensure a good join and hold the leader thread firmly under your thumb. (If you were to have the fibre and leader all going in the same direction this would make a worsted rather than woollen draw; *see* Chapter 3: Essential Spinning Techniques.)

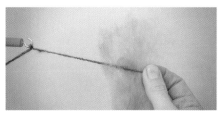

STEP 2   With your left hand twirl the spindle up towards and then away from you. In your right hand if you are still holding the leader thread securely with your thumb you will see fibres begin to attach to the lead thread as you put the twist in. It helps if you encourage the twist to move into the fibres by gently twirling the leader thread with your left hand. There is seldom enough twist for this to happen by itself, as twist naturally gravitates towards thin places.

STEP 3   Once the fibres are attached, gently release the pressure in your right hand and draw it away, leaving a few fibres free to form a roving (a tube or sausage shape of fibres) about 6 inches long. As you do this, twist will appear to jump into the thinner bunch of fibres and form a neck. Don't worry about the fat clump of fibres – these will be drawn out during the next stage.

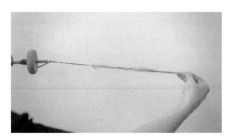

STEP 4   Still holding the spindle, continue to add twist and draw thread alternately. As you do so, try to feel for that stretchy elastic sensation that occurs when the balance of fibre and twist is just right and the fibres are able to form a thread. If it *feels* as though it might break, put in more twist. If it *looks* as if it will break, then rejoin again with more fibre placed crosswise as before. Hopefully you will experience a 'eureka' moment and draw a long thread!

STEP 5   Be careful not to draw the fibre out too thinly. Apart from the inconvenience of having to rejoin when you 'run out of fibre' (or you could say, it breaks!), it is more difficult to make a new join with a thin thread. Settle for a thick, strong thread at this stage. Unhook the leader and wind it onto the spindle stem, leaving enough to tie another half hitch and form the new leader thread.

STEP 6   Hold the leader thread in your right hand and roll the stem of the spindle down your left thigh to make lots of twist. It is important that it is your *left* thigh as this makes a Z twist.

STEP 7   Join on new fibres by laying the leader thread over them and holding with your thumb.

STEP 8   As the new fibres join, let in some twist and draw out a fat roving (a tube or sausage shape of fibres). Use each hand independently.

STEP 9   When you have a thick roving, stand up, roll the spindle down your left thigh to make more twist and quickly draw out the thread with both hands while the spindle spins in mid-air. Keep a close eye on the spindle as it will reverse and unspin all your good work once it loses momentum.

SPINNING ON A MODERN WHEEL

Modern wheels have an orifice through which the twisted yarn is threaded before being automatically wound onto removable bobbins. They incorporate bobbins and a flyer with hooks, which wraps yarn onto the bobbin for storage. They come in all shapes and sizes with either a single- or double-band drive mechanism. (The different types are illustrated and described in detail in Chapter 2.)

The single-band drive is considered easier for beginners. It incorporates a drive band that turns the flyer and a Scotch tension which enables the bobbins to fill automatically when required. The double-band drive is in fact a wheel with a single band that goes around twice! The double-band crosses at the top or bottom depending on the direction in which the wheel is turning, and this double band drives the bobbin and the flyer (wrapping) mechanism at the same time.

Whatever wheel you start with, it needs to be 'tuned' for optimum performance. This can be difficult for beginners as they don't know if the wheel is properly set up or how to do so if it is not, so if in doubt, ask an experienced spinner for help.

The Scotch tension on a single drive wheel enables the yarn to be stored on the bobbin without having to stop the wheel. It is recognizable as a thread which goes around the groove on a bobbin and works like a brake, causing the bobbin to turn more slowly or stop turning altogether. It looks like a piece of fishing line with an integral spring, and goes around the groove in the bobbin at the open end of the flyer and is adjusted by a knob on the wheel.

If there is too much tension on the leader thread it is the Scotch tension that needs loosening off. If the bobbin won't wind on then the Scotch tension is usually the reason why. The leader thread must always be under some degree of tension for the bobbin to wind on, but the less tension the better. This applies to the spinner as well as the wheel!

The widest groove offers the slowest turning speed. Beginners frequently make twist faster than they can use it.

Wheels need to be set to a low turning ratio by choosing the widest groove (circumference) on the flyer and, if there is a choice, the narrowest groove (circumference) on the wheel. New spinners always make twist faster than they can use it, so a low turning ratio helps minimize this problem. You could say a beginner's feet go too fast for their hands. So, try to turn the wheel as slowly as possible.

FEET FIRST

It is virtually impossible to concentrate on hands and feet at the same time. All beginners make too much twist as the wheel gathers momentum and takes control of the operation. The spinner must control the wheel, not the other way round. So before trying to work hands at the same time, take time to treadle the wheel without the distraction of trying to make yarn at the same time.

There are two points of pressure in treading: the heel and the toe; think of 'toe to go, heel to stop'. It is easier to get the wheel going than to stop it at a place where it will continue to turn in the correct, clockwise direction, when you are spinning.

A wheel such as an Ashford traditional is a good one to start with. It has a single drive band that goes around the wheel and Scotch tension controlled with a spring.

Practise stopping the wheel so that the crank is just before the vertical, then the wheel will turn in the correct direction for spinning (clockwise).

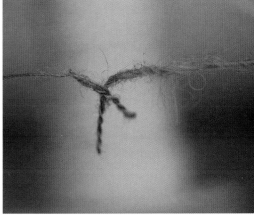

Squirmals are coils of singles thread created when the twist doubles back on itself.

Heel to stop...

Take the time to learn how to stop the wheel in the exact place you want. The wheel is driven by a crank (right-angled bend) that joins the axle to the footman. If the crank stops just before the footman reaches its highest point, the wheel will go backwards when you start it again.

This is frustrating and causes little 'squirmals' of yarn to build up on the thread as the tension is released on the leader thread. Squirmals are coils of singles thread created when the twist in a singles thread makes it double back on itself.

Ideally you will soon be able get the crank to stop with the footman just past the highest point (like the minute hand of a clock at 5 past the hour); the wheel will then be positioned ready to go in the correct, clockwise, direction when you start off again. Practise using your heel to stop the crank when it is in the exact place (5 past the hour) so that it will to set off in the correct (clockwise) direction when you need more twist.

It feels empowering to be able to turn the wheel back and forth at will, stopping and starting so the crank stops at whatever position you wish. This also saves having to take your hands off the spinning to flick a spoke to get it going. Remember to oil the wheel or adjust the drive band if it does not turn freely. A large well-balanced wheel will turn at least twelve revolutions when disconnected from the flyer and given a good flick.

...Toe to go

Once you can stop the wheel where you want, concentrate on the 'toe to go' aspect of treadling. Think in terms of creating enough momentum for the footplate to come back up under your foot. Tap and wait for the return; this is better than relying on speed to get the wheel to turn full circle. Going fast does not create impulsion, it just creates problems. What you are looking for is speed controlled by impulsion. It is rather like bouncing a ball so that it returns to your hand; if you just let the ball drop it runs out of energy and cannot bounce back up for the next tap. So try to create a tap-and-return feeling. Press the treadle and feel its energy return back for the next press. Now slow it right down to a steady pace. Treadling with the left foot seems to work best for right-handed spinners; right foot for left-handers.

TENSION

When spinning on a wheel the leader yarn must always be under some degree of tension. For new spinners the tension needs to be the minimum necessary to take yarn onto the bobbin. It should never feel like a pull. It is impossible to spin if the leader thread is being pulled out of the hand all the time.

On a wheel with a Scotch tension it is easy to see when the Scotch tension spring is too tight, which is helpful to beginners. On the more complex double-band drive wheel, the tension can only be felt and has to be adjusted by moving the mother-of-all away from, or closer to, the wheel (*see* Chapter 2). This alters the tension on the drive band and indirectly on the leader thread in the spinner's hand. The mother-of-all is the horizontal part onto which two upright support stands, called maidens, are mounted. Maidens hold the flyer, and the flyer in turn supports the bobbin.

A new spinner deserves a wheel that at least meets them half way, and the more simple the better. An experienced spinner can quickly feel and correct when a wheel is out of order, but this can be difficult for a beginner who has yet to learn 'feel',

Scotch tension: not enough.

Scotch tension: too much.

Scotch tension: just right.

and has no-one sitting alongside to help. However, all new spinners have to tackle the same issues by themselves eventually, and it is a good policy to blame the wheel if things are not going well. (The old adage, 'bad workmen blame their tools' is best ignored; in spinning it is the wheel that is to blame nearly all the time and the workman needs encouragement and support to learn how to fix it.)

One of the most common problems is to do with tension. Avoid setting up a tug of war with your wheel. If this happens, you may fall into the trap of only being able to make an inch or so of thread at a time, and end up hunched over the wheel engaged in what looks like a tug of war. The aim is to become a relaxed, as well as a productive, spinner!

Problems start when you use a wheel to make the twist, because the flyer mechanism won't work without tension. Without tension on the leader thread you can't spin on a traditional spinning wheel, the two are inseparable. The tension is essential to draw the thread onto the bobbin, it is not necessary in order to spin thread. The spinner must hold the tension and it is only when the tension is released that the bobbin winds on. The skill is to be able to manage the tension with one hand while drawing out the thread with the other.

When making a thread without a wheel. it is very easy to spin as there is no tension to contend with. While the spinning wheel is turning there is tension on the leader thread as twist is being made. To stop the tension the wheel must stop. To minimize the tension slacken off the Scotch tension knob/spring until there is just enough to draw thread onto the bobbin and no more.

Once a spinner can make twist, control it with one hand and draft fibre with the other it is easy – like riding a bicycle or swimming. Draw the thread and let it wind onto the bobbin, join on some more, let the twist in, draft a roving, draw the thread, feel it stretch, store on the bobbin. Hours can slip by without you noticing. But first you have to go through the learning curve, so be kind to yourself!

Just keep spinning, never mind the quality – that comes later – just aim to enjoy the feeling of it, mindful that spinning has been going on for centuries. Once upon a time everyone would have been familiar with spinning wheels and spindles; it has just missed a few generations.

So to reiterate, spinning is simply a matter of putting together fibre and twist. It takes place between the two hands: and a spinning wheel or spindle is only a means of making twist. The wheel does not control your spinning – unless you let it! It makes twist and you control the twist as well as the fibre. To spin on a wheel you need only to make twist at a rate at which it is used. So slowly, slowly turn the wheel and let it stop when things feel out of control. If it all starts to feel tense then stop treadling. Remember: the less tension there is, the better.

BETWEEN TWO HANDS

Always remember that spinning takes place between your two hands; the wheel only makes twist. Spinners control twist with one hand and fibre with the other. Which hand does which is a matter of preference when spinning on a modern wheel. Generally, but not always, right-handed spinners work with the left hand nearest the flyer orifice and the right hand holding the fibre and drawing the thread. Whichever is most comfortable is the correct way for any spinner.

When learning it can be helpful to think in terms of one hand doing something, then the other doing something. This is useful if you suddenly forget what to do next. Just think, 'which hand did something?' and then give the other something to do.

For example:
- Orifice hand – palm downwards: control the tension with three fingers nearest the orifice and let some twist build up.
- Fibre hand – loosely let out some fibres or 'draft a roving' as it is called.

The hand nearest the orifice controls the tension on the leader thread and the twist. The other hand draws the thread.

As the thread is drawn out, the fibres attenuate and start forming a thinner thread.

As thread is drawn out further, more twist is allowed in, which gives it strength.

- Orifice hand – roll some twist into the roving with thumb and forefinger (rolling up towards your body and then over and away) then continue to hold the twist so that only the amount you want is allowed into the roving.
- Fibre hand – draw out a thicker roving.
- Orifice hand – put in some more twist, run your fingers along the thread until both hands are together (to consolidate the twist).
- Fibre hand – allow the tension to wind thread onto the bobbin.

Repeat and enjoy!

WHEN IT FALLS APART

Take a break. In any learning process the brain can only take in so much. If you don't want to walk away, then just go back to the last place in the previous pages where you felt comfortable and it all made sense. Make yarn without a wheel again. Blame the wheel – most of the time it is the wheel that is the problem.

Skip forward a few chapters, enjoy the images, read about choosing fibre or using colour and relax. Try to imagine what it

would feel like to be knitting your own hand-spun yarn. Or if you dare, just day-dream about how lovely it must feel to be spinning arm's-lengths of yarn with the wheel chug-chugging along in a steady, peaceful rhythm.

Everyone learns differently, and it's surprising how the brain seems to process new things overnight. How long did it take you to learn to drive a car? Give yourself time to learn, take it slowly and don't get over-tired.

WHAT TO SPIN

Although fleece straight from the sheep (raw) is what often triggers the idea of spinning in the first place, it is rarely suitable to learn on. There is a huge difference in quality both within the breeds and within each fleece, and raw fleece can also become quite smelly, particularly in a warm room! Chapter 5 covers in detail the fleece and fibres that are available for hand spinning and the properties to look for in raw fleece – and more importantly what to avoid.

The concern here is to identify fibre suitable for learning with. Ideally this will be commercially prepared fibre rovings.

Clean, fairly fine, fleece which is free from contaminants such as straw or grass is the second choice. From the outset choose a quality fibre to learn with; inferior fibre can only ever make inferior yarn, even in experienced hands. Learners deserve something that meets them half way, not a battle to see who is the most tenacious, the fibre or the spinner.

You won't find an experienced spinner wasting time on fleece that is only fit for the compost heap (wool, being protein, makes good compost and helps water retention if dug straight into the ground at more than a spade's depth).

When you set out to spin it makes sense to make it as easy as possible. As a commodity wool is not expensive so choose the best – even for learning. 100g

Clean, easy-to-spin wool, such as this commercially prepared Blue-faced Leicester roving, is ideal for learning.

TROUBLE SHOOTING – THE WHEEL

Leader thread pulls in too strongly   Tension is the most common problem. Too much tension and the leader thread pulls in too strongly.

Thread won't wind onto the bobbin   Too little or no tension and the thread won't wind on to the bobbin and keeps twisting up. Thread might be caught on a hook, or wrapped around the flyer-spindle.

Making too much twist   Turn the wheel more slowly or stop it occasionally. Yarn is caught on a hook and can't wind onto the bobbin. Yarn is not threaded correctly through the orifice or is wrapped around the spindle. Tension thread is not in the bobbin groove.

Thread keeps snapping   Too much twist. Stop turning the wheel to allow hands to keep pace with speed of making twist. Slacken off the tension knob until the tension screw is just engaged, but not stretched.

Thread falls apart   Not enough fibre or not enough twist. Frequently caused by gripping fibres tightly. Think of supporting fibres rather than holding on to them.

Little twists of yarn   'Squirmals' appear on the bobbin: loss of tension in leader thread, usually because the wheel has turned backwards by mistake. Not a serious issue as it can be resolved in the plying stage.

Thread too thick   Thread not drawn out sufficiently before twist was allowed to run in.

Thread breaks at the join   Lay the leader thread right the way across the new fibres. Wait for fibres to wrap around the leader thread more fully before drafting the roving or drawing out the thread.

Thread is too fat, thin or lumpy   Fibre not suitable for a beginner or not suitably prepared.

Wheel hard to treadle   Oil moving parts. Drive band too tight; 1 inch play (i.e. it will move up or down about an inch) is usually sufficient.

Flyer intermittently stops going round while holding tension   Drive band too loose.

prepared fibre should not cost more than a cup of coffee or parking in a city car-park.

A commercially produced, fine-quality roving such as Blue-faced Leicester or merino is ideal to start with. It has the advantage of being clean and ready to spin with the fibres all lying in roughly the same direction. Spinning raw fleece or luxury camelid fibre such as alpaca is best left until later, along with choosing a wheel and equipment.

A staple length of each individual fibre of between 3 and 5 inches long is ideal for hand spinning. Anything over a handspan (+/– 8 inches) is too long; less than 2 inches is too short and will make spinning unnecessarily difficult. If possible choose two slightly different colours that complement each other. Blue-faced Leicester comes in several naturally different colours. This makes it easier to see when a join is going to be successful. Later on it will help with learning to ply two single threads together to make a stable yarn, as the two different colours show up the amount of twist in your final yarn.

No carding or preparation is necessary to spin rovings. Simply separate a few fibres by holding the roving along its length and gently easing off a few fibres from the end across the width. If the fibres are difficult, move your hands further apart to a distance greater than the staple length.

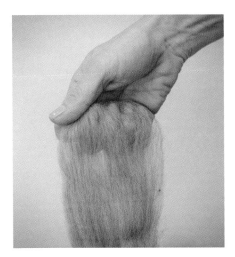

Pull off a few fibres very gently with hands far apart.

Spinning is a calm and peaceful process. (In the background is hand-spun raised-leaf work, knitted by R. Willatts.)

TAKE A MEDITATIVE BREAK

Learning to spin is demanding and far more difficult if your head feels like a jungle full of chattering monkeys. Turning a wheel slowly with the treadle is a very soothing distraction and can help clear the mind. Time spent in preparation is never wasted. Before even thinking about the practicalities of spinning, sit down at your wheel, on a chair with arms if possible. Make no plans to spin, just sit in a comfortable but alert position and begin treadling in a steady rhythmic manner with the wheel turning clockwise. Rest your elbows on the arms of the chair and let your hands lie palm downwards on your thighs. It is easier to feel the nuances of the movement with bare feet. Right-handed spinners usually find using the left foot to treadle has a more calming effect. The aim is to be comfortable and in a meditative, as opposed to anticipatory, frame of mind.

Once the wheel is going at a steady pace, close your eyes and concentrate on the steady, repetitive and rhythmic movement. As thoughts come into your head, gently let them go and pay attention to the treadling, focusing on the movement. Like your breathing, which is effortless, just let the wheel keep turning and feel comfortable in it. Spinning is a peaceful process, so a calm, peaceful mind is a helpful companion in the learning process. Ten minutes is all it takes.

LEARNING IS DEMANDING

When you are learning to spin, the aim is to learn how to control twist with one hand, fibre with the other, and manage a wheel or spindle at the same time – a tall order! Try to avoid making unnecessary demands such as consistent quality at this stage; correcting mistakes is a waste of learning time. For now, just concentrate on learning the technique – if you can bear to do so, just let mistakes go on to the bobbin and forget all about them. You have a lifetime to learn quality control, so just be content that you are spinning your own yarn and remember that it may turn out better than you think. To make a yarn you need two single threads from two bobbins, twisted together in the opposite direction; hopefully the rough on one bobbin will pair up with the smooth on the other! Your first spinning is extremely valuable, as it will show how you have improved... one day.

2 Bewitched and Bewildered
Spinning methods and wheels

It is so easy to become bewitched by beautiful wheels, and bewildered by conflicting advice. This chapter describes some of the difficulties beginners encounter and offers advice on how to avoid, or overcome, them. It gives an overview of various spinning wheels and devices and how they are used, the aim being to encourage independent thinking, competence and discernment.

Once upon a time, there was not much choice about what to spin on or, indeed, whether to spin or not. Spinning was just a part of life. Today, the choice of what to spin on, and what to spin, is considerable and the options are increasing all the time – as are the sources of advice and information. Unfortunately, for those researching online, there is no easy way to distinguish between what is generally accepted as 'received wisdom', and what is sometimes nothing more than personal opinion.

It is unreasonable to expect a complete beginner to make an informed choice about wheels and equipment. It takes time for a spinner's personal style and preference to develop, and such things continue to change as time goes on. Most people would not consider choosing a car at least until they have passed the driving test, so why buy a wheel?

Many of us are lured by old spinning wheels, particularly those that look fragile, unusual or reminiscent of fairytales. Love them by all means, but don't buy one to learn on, as it may make demands beyond your current skill level. What often happens in this situation is that many potentially competent spinners get stuck in the habit of making 2 inches of worsted yarn at a time, because that is the only way they can cope with the wheel. Once settled in this self-limiting comfort zone, many naturally gifted and creative spinners never develop their true potential, whether through lack of knowledge, skilled help or aspiration.

'Not on a wheel like the ones you usually see today!' The very old great wheels had a pointed spindle, which was kept very sharp, but modern wheels don't have them!

Scientific minds would refute it, but empirical evidence suggests that people find the right wheels, or maybe wheels find people, too often for it to be a coincidence. Just as in life, if you really want something to happen, it will – eventually. When you see a spinner with the right wheel for them, it shows. Everything flows, as with a musician playing a favourite instrument; the harmony is there, and the joy is unmistakable.

There are so many choices facing a would-be spinner:

- Should I choose a single or double drive-band wheel?
- Would I be better with an integral wheel?
- Single or double treadle?
- Electric spinner?
- What is a charkha?
- Is it wiser to start with a top or bottom whorl drop spindle, or Turkish? And what is the difference, anyway?

All of these questions will be answered below.

By far the most popular and successful wheel in living memory is the single drive-band Ashford Traditional. First made in New Zealand in the early 1940s, it is still available in much the same design today – although it now has all the benefits of technology, such as sealed bearings. These wheels are a good choice for beginners as they are easy to control and very little goes wrong with them. They are less costly than many wheels and suitable for spinning any type of yarn; new and used ones are readily available, along with spare bobbins, accessories and parts if required.

Far better to choose something tried and tested to learn on and leave making what you hope will be a lifetime purchase until you have the experience with which to choose.

AVOID GETTING IN A SPIN

All spinners make twist faster than they make yarn to start with. Don't worry about it! It is better to have too much twist than too little at the early stage. Remember that spinning by hand is an organic process so do not be too critical about what you produce.

Spinners are not machines and enthusiasm will soon wear off if you try to spin yarn to a precise number of twists per inch because you perceive this to be 'spinning properly'. Becoming a hand spinner is a far bigger thing than mimicking bought yarn.

Do not waste quality time worrying about the precise number of twists per inch in your yarn. It simply does not matter. How would you measure it anyway? Would you measure every inch of the 500-yard skein of finished yarn? And, if you were obsessive enough to do so, would you throw out the whole lot because a 1-inch section had a twist missing? No. We are talking spinning here, not precision engineering!

Getting bogged down in mathematical formulae and trying to meet some-one else's specification as to what your yarn should be like will kill your creativity, stone dead. As long as a yarn is fit for the purpose, then it is at least good enough – and at best, perfect.

BE KIND TO YOURSELF

Spinning is creative: you are not just making the yarn, but designing it too, so go where your heart lies. If you do not like what you are spinning, using, seeing, feeling, smelling and producing, then change it. There is no reason to force yourself to follow someone else's idea of what to spin. Be yourself, enjoy the natural products of the world, and create yarn in a mindful way and take pleasure in the process. The thinking spinner will wish to acquire as much information and as wide a skill-base as they can and then make their own, well-informed choices.

The real issue for a spinner is to be able to spin yarn that is fit for their own purpose. For this, the yarn needs to be spun and tested and the spinning adjusted as necessary. The techniques described here are aimed at empowering new spinners to reach their own unique potential, and avoid becoming fixated on the orifice as if it were grindstone. That is fine for a machine, but not for today's intelligent, mindful hand spinners.

By taking the time to learn just one or two spinning techniques, a spinner can make any sort of yarn they like, at very little cost, and gain many times the satisfaction.

Spinning is not meant to be about meeting rigid, mathematical and exacting criteria as was forced upon beginners in the past – and is sadly still sometimes accepted as the only standard of achievement or excellence. What about art? What about 'fit for purpose'? What about performance? What about bringing joy? Surely it is a waste of our humanity to spend a spinning lifetime doing exactly what a machine can do? Better to concentrate on, and take the time to learn, methods of spinning that produce yarns best suited to specific purposes.

Spinning techniques draw on the lessons of ancient history and today embrace new fibres and technology such as the e-spinner and blending board, the purpose being to free up, help and inspire every new spinner to reach their own unique potential. How many people would choose a plastic coated white-sliced loaf, in preference to one handed to them by the baker, wrapped in paper still warm from the oven? Every loaf is different but it is still bread; every 'hand-spun' is different but it is the same wool. It is all a question of personal values and perception: the secret is personal value, not public perception.

Although there are no definitive rules for spinning, there is some received wisdom. For example, a yarn intended for socks will need to be very robust in order to withstand, when walking, the intense pressure and friction exerted underfoot and at the toes and heels. Yarn for a fisherman's gansey also needs to be fine and strong, but it needs to be have lots of closely packed fibre in order to withstand wind and repel water spray at sea. But, for less extreme conditions, a soft and springy yarn is what is needed for a warm pullover or hat with good insulation properties, which breathes and feels cosy without feeling rough on the skin.

New fibres, new dyes, new equipment – did spinners ever have such opportunities?

Alternatively, you could be spinning a particular fleece, or mixing fibres and colours just for experimental purposes, or spinning for artistry – this calls for an entirely different approach. Spinners need to feel free to push boundaries and explore new fibres, experimenting with colour and creating unique textures and yarns that money can't buy.

One of the joys of spinning is being able to produce lots of different yarns knowing they will give a lifetime of pleasure – not just to the owner of the end product, but to the spinner who created it!

Wool is extremely versatile, whether for art, luxury wear or making life bearable in cold or temperate climates. We can take advantage of this versatility in both practical and creative ways by choosing techniques such as worsted draw, long draw or core-spinning – as the need arises. And there are many more fibres other than sheep fleece, as we shall discover in Chapter 5. Whatever the purpose, there is always an appropriate spinning technique or skill suited to it.

Hand-spun sleeveless pullover – Hebridean fleece.

KEEP IT SIMPLE – START WITH A SPINDLE

The drop spindle is great way to start spinning and they are easily obtainable at comparatively little cost. A new spindle will cost a lot less than a meal out, and will last a lot longer! Once you understand the technique, and can spin on a drop spindle, then spinning on a wheel can be a natural development.

On the drop spindle, spinning and winding on are two separate movements. Unlike on a spinning wheel, there is no continuous tension to deal with on the

Top whorl spindle – an ideal way to start.

Secure leader thread with a half-hitch.

leader thread, just the weight of the spindle. Wheels tend to run away with beginners, but the drop spindle is infinitely controllable. And control is just what you need when learning something new.

The top whorl is the first choice to learn on, as it twirls easily by hand without the thread getting in the way; it rolls along the table-top and, when you get going, rolls down your left thigh for spinning and right thigh when it comes to plying. Other spindles may work just as well – you won't know until you try – but you can be certain that a drop spindle will not run away with you, making twist faster than you can use it, like a wheel does when you first start.

SPINDLES FOR ALL SEASONS

There are many, many different types of drop spindles. Some are used in suspension with the thread that is being made, and others are suspended and supported on a polished surface.

The three types of spindle most commonly seen are the **top whorl**, **bottom whorl** and **Turkish spindles**.

The top whorl spindle has a hook in the top of the stem and the whorl is positioned towards the top as the name implies. Lightweight top whorl spindles are the easiest, and one of the lightest is Ashford's 50, which weighs less than 20g.

The bottom whorl spindle sometimes has a notch cut into the top of the stem where the leader thread is tied with a hitch.

The benefit of the Turkish spindle is that, with weights added to the outer part of the whorl sections, centrifugal force increases the length of time that the spindle spins. Thread is stored on the spindle by winding over two parts and under the next so that fibre builds up in the hollow section. The spindle is dismantled to free up a ball-shaped batch of singles thread. Two or three of these singles can then be plied together.

From left: bottom, top, and bottom whorl spindles.

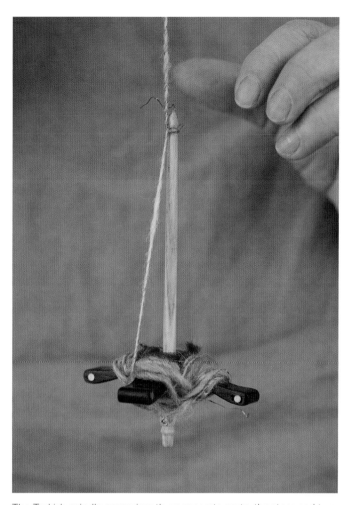

The Turkish spindle comprises three separate parts: the stem and two shaped parts which slide over the stem and lock together to form the whorl.

Some Turkish spindles can be taken apart and concealed in a bag when travelling light!

SPINNING ON A TOP WHORL SPINDLE

The top whorl spindle allows you to understand and practise quietly and calmly. When you have got the gist of it on the table top, then you can put all the movements together. Before you know it, you will be standing up and rolling the spindle down your thigh, making lovely lengths of singles thread.

The method taught here is the traditional woollen, or long draw technique which yields arms' lengths of springy singles thread, ideal for knitting and crochet. It is the oldest known method of spinning and is a very satisfying, speedy and yet relaxing way to spin.

It is also very elegant to watch. And there is the added bonus that with the long draw technique, one can spin any fibre and spin on any wheel – well worth the effort of learning!

Long draw technique

1. To start long draw on a top whorl spindle, tie a leader thread tightly round the stem using a clove hitch (or two half hitches) which will not slip, but can be slipped off when necessary.

2. Take the spindle in your left hand and lay it down on a table top – a cloth on the table is helpful if the table is polished and slippery.

3. Hold the leader thread across a few fibres, half way down the staple. Lay the leader well over to ensure a secure join, and hold it firmly in place under your thumb.

4. With your left hand, twirl the drop spindle up towards and then away from you to put in the twist (Z) until you see the fibres attach to the leader thread.

5. Draw out your right hand for about 6 inches and put in more twist until you see a *neck* form (where all the twist is in one place).

6. Still holding the spindle, draw out again to about 12 inches of thread, feeling the elasticity as fibres slide over each other. NB: If it *feels* as if it will break, put in more twist. If it *looks* as if it will break, then rejoin in with more fibre – crosswise, of course.

7. When you have a fairly thick, even thread, put in more twist to stabilize it by rolling the spindle on the table or twirling in your hand.

8. Wind thread on to the spindle.

9. Repeat and enjoy!

The next stage is to combine the movements into a cohesive whole, using each hand independently:

1. Hold the leader thread in your right hand and roll the bobbin down your left thigh (this always makes Z twist.)

2. Hold the twist and spindle in your left hand while you join on the new fibres. As they join, let in a little bit of twist and draw the thread.

3. When you have a strong roving, stand up, roll the spindle down your thigh to create more twist and draw the thread thinner. The advantage of a light spindle is that the thread is less likely to break before sufficient twist is added due to its own weight. However, bear in mind that as the spindle gets more full it will become heavier.

With just a little bit of practice you will be able to put in twist and draw at the same time, as Abby Franquemont demonstrates so beautifully and clearly in her book, *Respect the Spindle*.

Spinning is quality time and too good to waste on unsuitable fibre.

ACHIEVING CONSISTENCY: THE EYEBALL TEST

It is extremely difficult to achieve precise control over every inch of yarn you produce, particularly if you are creating 18 inches of yarn at a time! It is rarely necessary, and certainly not fun. Twist has a habit of evening itself out along a thread, so adjustments every inch or so are irrelevant unless carried out at the point where the thread enters the orifice. There is also loss of twist when plying the singles when the wheel is turned in the opposite direction. So, it is not an exact science.

However, some method of achieving consistency is essential. This is where the 'eyeball test' comes in: first, make a sample, measure and test it. This may mean wrapping it around a yarn gauge or actually knitting a sample. When your sample is satisfactory, tie it on to your wheel.

Stop every so often to take a close look – with a magnifying glass if necessary – and see how your spinning compares with your *control sample*. When spinning lots of yarn over a long period of time, it is easy to find yourself spinning thicker or thinner. Hence a reference point is essential; in short, just make a thread that fits the purpose and match it.

SHOULD I BE SPINNING THIS?

When things are not going well, this question is well worth asking.

All too often, spinners get stuck with something they feel they have to spin: 'My mother-in-law gave it to me'; 'It's my friend's sheep'; 'I bought it and I don't really like it'; 'I've got to do this before I can start on what I really want to be doing' … the reasons go on for ever.

But there is seldom a good reason to be wasting your quality time spinning something you don't like. Not every sheep has fleece worthy of spinning, and if it doesn't feel right then forget it. Discernment in choosing fleece comes with experience; advice on this is given in Chapter 4.

CHOOSING A WHEEL

The purpose of this section is to highlight the many differences between wheels. It starts with points to watch out for when buying a used wheel, as this is often where mistakes are made. References are to wheels by genre rather than models offered by a particular manufacturer.

Spinners may be inspired to learn because they have sheep or alpaca, or they might know of a wheel that is not being used. In some cases it feels as if a wheel 'finds' a potential spinner, as if it were looking for a new owner – rather like a stray cat – and in other cases a spinner simply goes looking. There is usually a catalyst to spark the adventure.

Unfortunately, there are plenty of wheels for sale that are no good for spinning on. The trick is to be able to spot the 'decorative' models and avoid them.

The following checklist may be helpful when viewing used wheels:

1. If there is no known manufacturer's name on the wheel, be very cautious – or just forget it. There are many wheels, sold many times, that have never spun a yarn and never will. A maker's name is easy to research on the Internet. Popular current manufacturers include Ashford, Kromsky, Lendrum, Majacraft and Schacht.

2. What size is the orifice? If it is less than 1cm in diameter, avoid buying it, as it is probably designed for spinning flax, not wool.

3. Are there any bobbins? Unless there are at least three, spinning will soon become tedious. Refuse offers to make them – they are seldom satisfactory. If bobbins are not commercially available, forget the wheel.

4. Does the framework supporting the wheel wobble about when you put pressure on it? It needs to be sturdy, but you may be able to rectify this.

5. Does the wheel turn true, i.e. when viewed from the side, does it appear to wobble as it turns? This may or may not be a problem, but why consider a potential problem when there are plenty of wheels on offer?

6. Is the drive band of the wheel perfectly aligned with the flyer pulley? Can you make it so? If not, the drive band will fly off as soon as the wheel gathers speed.

7. Remove the drive band and give the wheel a spin. If it does not turn freely, for at least ten revolutions, then you will soon tire of treadling it.

8. Remove the Scotch tension and spin the bobbin. It should turn freely. If not, you will not be able to spin on it at all.

SINGLE DRIVE-BAND WHEEL

A single drive band is exactly that: one band that goes around the wheel and the flyer pulley. Confusingly, a double drive band is also a single band but it goes twice around the wheel and the flyer pulley. A traditional single drive-band wheel is easy to learn on. Commonly seen with a single footplate, these have a large accessible wheel which is made with a generous amount of wood which aids momentum, i.e. once the wheel is turning, it keeps turning more easily than a smaller wheel

WHEEL RATIOS AND TWIST

The speed of the wheel regulates how much twist ends up in a given length of yarn. Using the lowest ratio of twist per revolution of the wheel will maximize control. It is easy to speed up, but not so easy to keep a slow, steady pace.

To find the lowest ratio, set the drive band on the largest whorl on the flyer and smallest diameter on the wheel (note that not all wheels have this option).

An Ashford traditional wheel has a ratio of 6.5 twists per revolution of the wheel at its lowest setting. There is no need to get obsessive about twists per inch. Just check your spun yarn every so often and speed up or slow down according to what your yarn looks like.

A wheel with a low turning ratio is ideal for beginners who invariably make twist faster than they make thread. A wheel with a turning ratio of say 6.5 is a good starting point. This means that for each turn of the large wheel, 6.5 twists go into the thread being made. A high ratio might be 17.5, which is suitable for spinning fine thread or fast plying.

The ratio of a wheel can be calculated by measuring the diameter of the large wheel and the diameter of the pulley on the flyer, where the drive band goes. Divide the larger diameter by the smaller diameter to give the ratio.

For example:
Diameter of wheel (55cm) ÷ Diameter of flyer pulley (9cm) = Ratio 6.1

As you become more skilled, you will gain increased control over the treadle and the speed at which twist is made. And, at this stage, your hands are increasingly busy too, so the more you can control the wheel without hands, the easier and more relaxing your spinning will become. Learning to treadle slowly can be a meditative experience.

would. Look for a simple Scotch tension, called a brake band, made of two springs and fine acrylic cable adjusted by a simple knob. The wheel needs to be robust and tolerate being transported. Wheels often end up in and out of cars, wedged between child seats, laid flat out over wellies, buckets, and cat baskets, and, mercifully, sometimes sedately strapped in with seat belts like a venerable great aunt.

A single drive-band wheel always has a Scotch tension which, when it is engaged, stops the bobbin from turning while the flyer continues around it, laying down newly made thread onto the bobbin. The tension can almost be set by seeing when the spring engages – if it looks in the least bit stretched, there is too much tension and that will make life difficult for new spinners.

Scotch tension units frequently have two springs, one either side of the bobbin. The spring on the left comes into play when spinning Z (or clockwise from where the spinner is sitting) so that is the one to watch when setting up. The spring to the right of the bobbin comes into play when plying. Many older wheels don't have a plying spring. The mechanics are simple. The acrylic line creates drag as it goes over the bobbin. Hence, it is better to put the thin end of the bobbin into the flyer first, and let the wider end maximize drag as it makes more contact along the groove.

Wheels can have cord, string or thick acrylic flexible polycord drive bands. String drive bands need about an inch of play on them for easy treadling (if you press on the string it will move up or down for about an inch before resisting). If the drive band is too tight it makes treadling hard, and the wheel will stop at every given opportunity, which is frustrating.

A large, easily accessible wheel is easy to set off in the correct, clockwise or Z direction (*see* Chapter 6). Just think of stroking the wheel downwards with the right hand. You can not stroke it anticlockwise (S) because the drive band gets in the way.

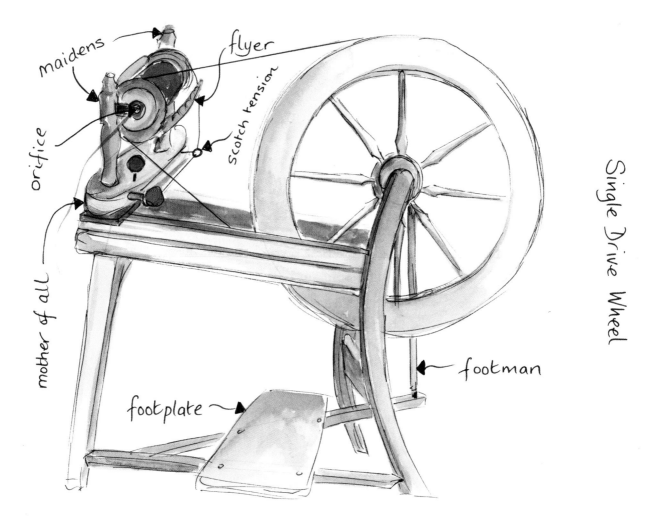

maidens

flyer

orifice

Scotch tension

mother of all

footplate

footman

Single Drive Wheel

VERTICAL INTEGRAL AND COLLAPSIBLE WHEELS

There are also single or double treadle spinning wheels which have a small integral wheel standing directly above the legs. The flyer is usually mounted directly above the wheel or to one side, which means that it may be higher than is comfortable for some spinners.

Whereas the orifice is situated to the left of the spinner on a traditional wheel, here the spinner sits directly in front of the orifice. This is a matter of personal preference.

The dimensions of such wheels are often smaller than the traditional 'wheel on the right, flyer on the left' type, described above. One advantage is that such wheels generally have a smaller 'footprint', which is an important factor if it is to be used in a small home or confined space.

Vertical wheels frequently come with a double treadle – two footplates – so both feet are used to drive the wheel. This suits many people very well. A wheel with a double treadle is also useful as it is possible to stop and turn the wheel in the opposite direction without using your hands. Some spinners only feel comfortable when using both feet, and beginners often find it is easier to treadle slowly with two feet rather than one. Experienced spinners can treadle double treadle wheels with one foot.

Both the Lendrum and Ashford Joy are collapsible for easier transport and storage when not in use. Most single band drive wheels have the option of a large flyer and bobbin accessories suitable for making thick or fancy yarn. Some wheels, such as the Schacht, incorporate both a single and double band drive mechanism, and are collapsible.

TRADITIONAL DOUBLE DRIVE-BAND WHEEL

The traditional double drive-band wheel is easily recognizable as it has a large screw-in knob at the end of the stock, and a whorl on the far end of the flyer. Generally, such wheels have no Scotch tension mechanism, although it is possible to attach one. These wheels are often larger than single drives and have a wide groove in the wheel to accommodate the double band.

The double drive band goes around the spindle whorl at the opposite end from a single drive flyer, i.e. furthest away from the spinner at the far end of the bobbin. The drive band is actually one long single band which goes around the large wheel twice, once round the pulley on the bobbin, and once round the pulley on the whorl. There are usually two pulleys on the whorl, the larger for spinning and the

Vertical integral wheel.

smaller for either plying or for spinning a high twist, finer yarn.

Because the wheels are generally larger, the turning ratio is higher than a single drive, which makes the wheels more appropriate for spinning finer yarn that needs more twist. Double band drive wheels are not the ideal choice for a learner as there is no visible Scotch tension to adjust the speed of take up or tension on the leader thread.

With a double band drive, the thread is stored on the bobbin due to the drive band travelling round the bobbin and the flyer, taking up the difference when not slipping. The bobbin pulley is smaller and, hence, travels faster than the flyer. The tension, not the drive band, is controlled by releasing the lock underneath the stock and moving the mother-of-all along the stock by means of a knob at the end of the stock.

The spindle whorl is reverse-threaded. To change a bobbin on the double drive wheel, the whorl must be removed from the flyer and the drive band with it, making the change a slightly more complex manoeuvre than on a single drive mechanism.

Double drive bobbins are easily recognizable, as they have two pulleys at one end.

Spinning on a double drive-band wheel requires the spinner to make twist nearer to the speed at which it is used and enable the take-up.

The single drive wheel has the capacity to store made yarn on the bobbin at a faster rate than the double drive. However, the double drive wheel frequently has a much higher turning ratio.

ELECTRIC SPINNER

The electric spinner is not a wheel at all, but a flyer and bobbin driven at low *torque* (turning power). The Ashford e-spinner incorporates a sliding flyer with rings instead of hooks and large bobbins and large orifice so it is ideal for making fancy yarns that would otherwise get caught up on hooks. Although it has a low turning ratio, it can turn at high speed, so the options are manifold.

Electric spinners are lightweight and ideal for people with coordination difficulties. They take up very little space and can be used on boats, in caravans or mobile homes. Low voltage transformers and international electrical fittings are available on most spinners.

Small, portable and finely controllable, one would think the e-spinner to be

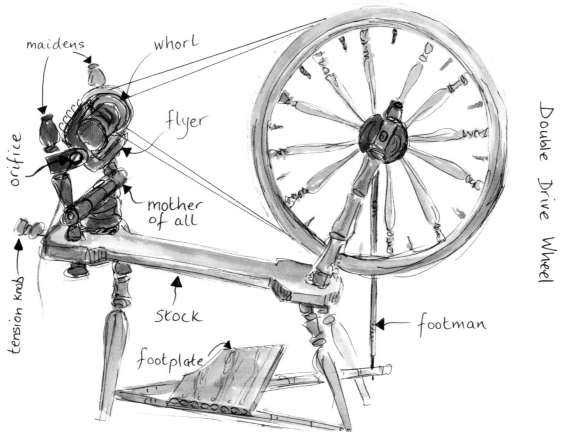

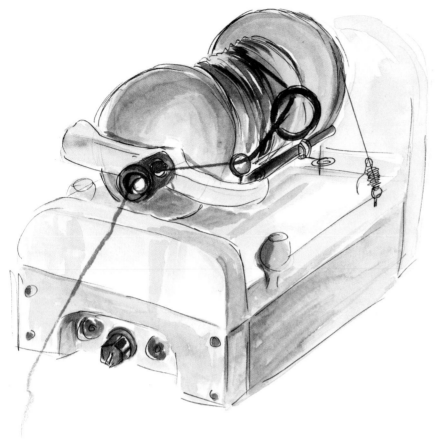

the outright winner. But it is not a wheel – and for some spinners the magic is missing if there is no wheel going round. The electric spinner has some unique benefits: it is a valuable learning/teaching device as it does not detract attention as it turns. The spinner rotates much more slowly than is achievable on a wheel and this allows time to demonstrate difficult and complex techniques slowly. Treadling can also be quite challenging to some beginners and another obstacle in the learning curve, and this can be conveniently set aside as a separate task with the e-spinner. Learning to spin and treadle at the same time asks a great deal from beginners.

The spinner may lack fairytale magic but, to the physically challenged, uncoordinated or even the plain lazy, the e-spinner is an absolute winner.

CHARKHA

The charkha was traditionally used for spinning cotton in the Far and Middle East. The cotton fibre was prepared into rolls, called punis, for spinning on the charkha. The wheel is commonly seen housed in a box and used flat on the ground, as famously used by Mahatma Ghandi. However, the modern charkha is mounted upright on a solid, fairly heavy frame.

Cotton needs lots more twist than wool to make yarn that has integrity. When spinning cotton, the fibre was traditionally prepared into punis, which were rolled around a dowel.

The charkha is ideal for spinning silk and cotton to a fine thread. There is no flyer or bobbin on the charkha – just a wheel with a crank handle that drives a very small diameter spindle.

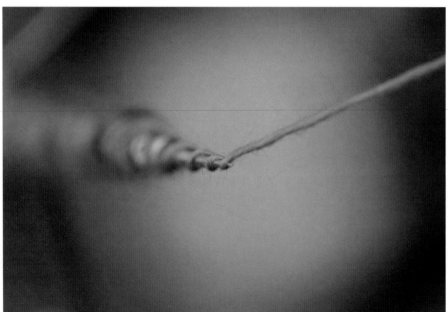

Spinning is 'off-the-point' on both charkha and great wheel – is this where the fairytale princess pricked her finger?

Thread is stored away from the point.

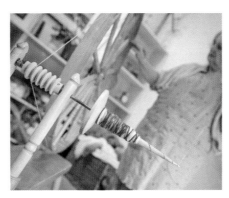

Spinning on a great wheel. The right hand turns the wheel, whilst the left hand draws the thread. The long draw is several feet long; this is the only technique with which to spin on a great wheel.

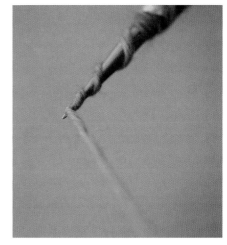

Twist enters the thread at the sharp point on both the great wheel and charkha.

Spinning on the charkha is normally done seated, as with modern wheels, but there the similarity ends. As the handle of the charkha wheel turns, the spindle turns very quickly due to its high ratio.

Twist is imparted as the spinner keeps the thread balanced on the point. A few fibres from the punis are attached to the leader thread and then drafted out.

When the thread is sufficiently drawn out, the wheel is stopped and reversed to release the thread from the tip of the spindle. The finished thread is then stored on the spindle stem away from the point.

The big issue, when spinning with a charkha, is that it makes twist very, very fast: at least ten times faster than a traditional wheel. So, if you want to spin wool, then the charkha is not the best option.

Both charkha and the great wheel require a similarly skilful approach as twist is made by spinning from a point, rather than through an orifice on a modern wheel. And only the left hand is available to draft the fibre, as the right hand is needed to turn the wheel. Hence, drafting and imparting twist takes place more or less at the same time in one swift long draw.

GREAT WHEEL

The great wheel, sometimes known as a walking wheel, is the oldest known wheel in the UK. Another lovely illustration of one can be seen in the Luttrell Psalter in the British Library (Lincolnshire, *c.*1320–40, British Library Add. MS 42130).

The great wheel was mounted on a bench that stood on legs and was several feet high. The traditional long draw method is the only means of spinning on a great wheel. Today, working great wheels are found principally in specialist spinning schools or heritage centres, as they are not easily accommodated in the modern home.

The great wheel is several feet in diameter, connected to a very much smaller spindle; hence, like the charkha, it makes twist very quickly. The distance between the drive wheel and spindle demands an accomplished skill level of long draw, using the left hand.

Spinning on a great wheel is always from a standing position and involves walking back and forth while turning the wheel with the right hand. The wheel is turned clockwise for spinning and temporarily reversed for winding on. Spinning is usually, but not necessarily, from loosely rolled bundles of wool called 'rolags' made with hand carders (*see* Chapter 5).

Drafting is with the left hand while the right hand turns the wheel. The spinner attaches a rolag to a short leader thread using the left hand and then walks backwards, drafting up to several feet of thread at a time. Obviously, this long draw method produces thread very quickly.

We know from Gervase Markham's book, *Countrey Contentments, or, The English Huswife* that long draw spinning was standard practice in 1623 when the book was published:

After your wool is thus mixed … you shall then spin it up on great wool wheels, according to the order of good housewifery.

3 Essential Spinning Techniques

In this chapter our rich heritage of traditional hand spinning methods is explained in detail, along with some new techniques. The rationale is to help and encourage serious spinners to learn new skills and techniques that will open up new horizons in their yarn design.

Thread is essentially fibre and twist carefully brought together so that the fibres are free to slip over each other (attenuate). This sounds very simple, yet there are many different ways to do this and this and each way has a profound influence on yarn design. Appearance, performance, texture, reaction to light and artistic merit – all of these change according to the way a fibre is spun.

Discussion throughout this chapter concerns the spinning of singles thread, spun in a clockwise (Z) direction then stored on a bobbin or spindle. This means always turning the wheel in a clockwise direction, or always rolling a top-whorl spindle down the left leg (*see* 'Y spin Z?').

Singles thread is unstable and needs to remain on the bobbin or spindle until it is plied to make a finished, stable yarn. Plying involves two or more singles threads that are twisted together in the opposite direction (S) to which they are spun (Z). The various plying techniques are explained in detail in Chapter 6: Plying.

Fibre, twist and tension can combine in countless different ways. For example, if the fibres are all the same length, combed parallel and twist is applied end on, i.e. at the tips of the fibre, the thread can be drawn under strong tension and will turn out thin, smooth and really strong.

Hand-spun yarn is free from commercial restraints.

Softly spun, hand-dyed merino/silk two ply.

Such thread is excellent for weaving or knitting socks where the yarn comes under friction and pressure inside a shoe. But such a yarn is not so good for a warm woolly pullover or hat; in this instance it is better if the fibres start off all jumbled up together so that air gets trapped as they fold over and attenuate. The result is a 'lofty' yarn that is soft, springy and feels warm and cosy to wear.

The direction in which the thread is drawn out when the fibre and twist come together in a loose roving profoundly effects the properties of a finished yarn.

Draw can either be towards, or away from the point where the twist enters the fibres. If the draw is coming from the point of twist, known as 'forward draw', it takes place over a short distance being limited by the distance between the fibre source and point of twist. In this way, the tension of the draw can be quite intense without the thread breaking.

When thread is held and the draw is made away from the point of twist and away from the wheel, known as 'long draw', the drawing distance can be anything from an arm's length, if the spinner is sitting, to a few paces, if standing. The longer draw allows for greater freedom of movement of fibres as they attenuate because there is no concentration of twist in a short area, as in forward draw. Twist is energy and flows or travels like electricity along a cable. Hence, in long draw, the tension needs fine, subtle adjustments to allow time for the twist and fibres to trap little pockets of air as they attenuate. The result is not as strong, but is warmer and more bulky.

THE ESSENCE OF HAND-SPUN YARN

Whereas hand spinning can be forward or long draw, commercial production is usually forward draw. Here, spinning bobbins create twist and draw in the thread at the same time. In commercial production loft is achieved by the careful choice of fleece, and mix of short and long fibres. There is no benefit in comparing commercial yarn with hand-spun yarn; the two are created for different reasons. Using commercial yarn as the benchmark is totally inappropriate, and can be disheartening for the beginner. When this happens the tendency is to aim for consistency and short forward draw, carefully controlling every few fibres as they are pulled onto the bobbin under tension in the commercial manner. It is wiser to adopt the habit of letting mistakes go and work at avoiding them happening in the first place, rather than to keep stopping and correcting errors.

Hand-spun yarn is free from the constraints of commercial production and this is one of the reasons to rejoice in it. When commercial suppliers try to mimic hand-spun the yarn is always very costly. While both are full of fun, commercial and hand-spun yarns are inherently different and the difference is what counts.

Machine spinning changed life dramatically in the 1800s and played a major part in the Industrial Revolution. It changed not only *where* it was done (moving from the cottage to the 'satanic' mills); it also changed the *method* of spinning and the way in which fibre and twist were put together (forward draw). Even today, this is one of the most misunderstood aspects of hand spinning.

The ubiquitous short forward draw is all too often the only method spinners consider today, traditional long draw being forgotten or considered elitist or too difficult to learn – if it is considered at all – even though this was the standard hand spinning method for centuries beforehand. Learning to spin short forward draw, on a scale of difficulty 1–10 is probably only 2 or 3. Learning long draw is more like 7 or 8 because greater control of twist and fibre is required and learning to do both at the same time asks more of a beginner.

Only one of the early commercial spinning machines, Crompton's mule, used the long draw technique. Here, each length or roving was drawn out, away from the point of twist, then wound back onto the bobbin, creating an intermittent forwards and backwards movement. Not surprisingly, this was superseded by the faster Arkwright forward draw device with its smooth, slick, all-in-the-same direction action.

The hand spinner, unaffected by commercial restraints, can create short runs of totally unique yarns drawing on fibre, colour, structure and texture. There has never been a time in history when such a variety of fibre and spinning equipment to spin on has been available. Nor has there been a time when so many people have sufficient leisure time with which to explore the craft.

It is helpful to remember that there is an inverse relationship between fibre and twist. Spinning thick yarn requires much less twist than spinning thin. But when fibre is sparse and spinning gets thin a lot more twist is needed. As noted before, most beginners make twist faster than they can make yarn, so it is helpful to stop the wheel every so often, or select a low turning ratio where possible, whatever the spinning method.

Smithfield Decretals (Decretals of Gregory IX) entitled 'An Amorous Encounter'. Originally produced in France, but probably illustrated in London *c.*1340. The British Library.

LONG DRAW, OR WOOLLEN YARN

The term 'long draw' refers to a method of production and 'woollen' refers to the nature of the yarn it yields. Woollen yarn was traditionally produced using the long draw technique as demonstrated in medieval manuscripts. It describes a yarn that is lofty and typically but not exclusively used for knitting, crochet or weft yarn. The opposite of a woollen yarn is worsted yarn, which is typically but not exclusively used for weaving and hardwearing knitwear.

Long draw yields a springy, lofty and bouncy yarn. Because it contains lots of air, the yarn has good insulation properties and is ideal for knitted and crocheted garments or soft furnishings such as throws and blankets. It is also useful for weaving on the rigid heddle loom.

Long draw is a very old technique; it was known in France as long ago as the fourteenth century, as shown in the 'Amorous Encounter'. Here the spinner is standing at a great wheel with what looks like several feet of thread between her hand and the point of the spindle. Behind her is a man whose interests clearly do not include the spinning wheel, and the spinner herself is not paying much attention to her work either!

Long draw is a very relaxing and satisfying way to spin as it produces longer lengths of thread at a time rather than just an inch or two. The most obvious difference between long draw and any other method is that the drawing is made between the spinner's two hands away from the orifice, not towards it. The spinner can draw out the length of the arm if required. The other critical difference is the way the fibre is presented to the leader thread at right angles, rather than end on.

Long draw is all about managing twist: withholding or allowing it into a drafted roving and then drawing out the thread away from the wheel, before allowing it to wind onto the bobbin.

When the balance between fibre and twist is just right, the thread feels as if it is stretching like chewing gum, but does not draw back like elastic. So, how do you know when the balance is right? This is clear to see as the twist will form a neck, jumping over a few fibres leaving a thick place behind it and, when this happens, the thread can be drawn out. Then let in more twist, then a little more draw, alternating until you have the desired thickness of thread.

Remember that this thread is only half of your finished yarn – at the most, as it will need to be plied (*see* Chapter 6).

The technique requires only enough tension for the flyer to wind onto the bobbin. Hence, it feels a very relaxing way to spin and the twist is free to move along the roving. Sometimes, too much twist will enter into the thread and it will be impossible to draw out further. When this happens, engage the brain, not the muscles, or it will simply break. If too much twist has been allowed to enter, then it can be let out at the fibre end or untwisted with the hand nearest the orifice.

Sometimes, only one or two reverse twists is all that is needed to release the fibres. Holding the fibres with palm facing downwards allows for the tension to be controlled with three fingers, leaving the thumb and forefinger free to roll or back-off the twist by drawing your finger back towards you over your thumb. This is usually enough to loosen the fibres and allow more drawing. Letting out more

LONG DRAW

For a right-handed spinner, the right hand holds the fibre, and the left hand controls twist. For left-handed spinners (instructions in brackets), the left hand holds the fibre, and right hand controls twist.

STEP 1   Attach leader thread: hold the fibre, or rolag, in your right (or left hand) and lay the leader thread over it, holding it in place with your thumb. The leader thread will only feel as though it is coming under tension if the wheel is turning and creating twist.

STEP 2   With the left (or right) thumb and forefinger about 5 or 6 inches away from the orifice, pinch and hold the leader thread so that no twist can get past. Turn the wheel several times and make and store the twist in the 5–6 inches thread between your hand and the orifice. With the left (or right) hand, roll some twist into the roving, rolling it up towards your body and away from you (Z) continue to hold the twist.

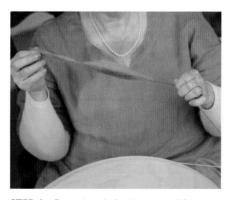

STEP 3   Slowly, draft out a roving of fibres by letting them freely out of your right hand and draw away until you see the twist jump into the roving forming a neck. Hands will be 6–8 inches apart at this stage. Twist never wants to flow into a fat fibre mass but prefers to sit in the thin places, hence, in the first instance, encourage twist to roll into the roving.

STEP 4   Draw hands further apart (12 inches or more), and as soon as the neck forms, carefully roll in more twist. As you do this, twist will flow into the thin places more easily, without the need to keep rolling it between fingers and thumb. The fibres will slip over each other forming a smooth thread which feels stretchy.

STEP 5   Alternately, add more twist and draw in separate movements, until the yarn is the desired thickness, then add sufficient twist for strength.

fibre also allows twist to move along a greater length, freeing up more fibre as it does so.

What determines a woollen long draw is the way in which fibre is presented to the twist: at right angles to the leader thread. This is like a bridge crossing a river – one flows one way and the other goes across it at right angles. The draw takes place between the spinner's hands and the direction is always made away from the wheel, never towards it.

The long draw can be up to an arm's length at a time on a spinning wheel and several feet on a great wheel.

Twist needs to be carefully controlled, letting in just a little at a time until the fibres can begin to align themselves throughout the length of the roving. This creates the characteristic woollen thread with a bouncy airy feel to it known as 'loft'. This loft or bouncy feel is not fully apparent until the yarn is plied and finished.

It is commonly thought that long draw can only be done from specially prepared light rolls of wool known as 'rolags' but this is not true (*see* Chapter 5: fibre preparation/rolags). Spinning from a rolag is easier, however, as the structure of a rolag ensures crosswise (bridge over the river) presentation of the fibre when the leader thread is joined to one end. It was also the traditional way it was done, as evidenced by the 'Amorous Encounter' featured earlier, and again in the fourteenth-century Luttrell Psalter, which can be seen on the British Library website.

WORSTED DRAW

A worsted yarn is smooth, strong and solid. As it can be spun very fine, this makes it an excellent choice for weaving as it will pass through heddles with minimum resistance and wear (shredding). It can also be spun very finely for projects where the pursuit of excellence is the primary purpose (see the Shetland Hap shawl in Chapter 10). A worsted yarn can be knitted or woven tight enough to prevent water ingress.

Worsted draw can be either from a few fibres, combed to be lying parallel with each other in a bunch, or from combed fibre pre-drafted into a fine roving.

Generally, a worsted thread is thinner than a woollen draw singles and contains much more twist. It is usual to spin with a higher tension from the flyer than for long draw and this can be used to assist with the drafting and drawing out processes. The aim is to create a smooth yarn with plenty of twist, which is fine and, proportionately, very strong for its weight.

Alternatively, the draw can be made away from the wheel allowing twist into the roving in a smooth controlled movement and drawing away at the same time (as in long draw). This is particularly useful for long stapled fleece such as Wensleydale or Leicester Longwool. If the fibres are shorter than 5–7 inches, the forward draw is usually easier.

The direction of draw, for worsted, can be either short forward or long draw away from the point of twist, but in all other respects it is the opposite of woollen draw, yielding a strong, smooth, fine yarn with fibres tightly packed.

To spin worsted draw, fibres need to be carefully prepared and laid out parallel to each other. Fibres are joined to the leader at the tip or cut end. Like fish swimming up a river, everything travels in the same direction. The fibres are not free to fold over themselves but are carefully controlled and fed in so that they lie close to each other, smoothly packed together to form a dense thread.

This affects both the appearance and performance of the thread, as well as the texture. Generally, longer fibres, 5–12 inch staple, can easily be spun in the worsted technique by beginners and even silk, which comes in a much longer filament, is fairly easy to handle and less likely to break.

WORSTED DRAW

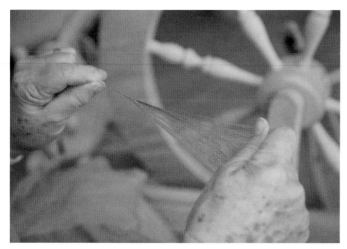

STEP 1 Hold fibres in the fibre hand – the one furthest away from the orifice or spindle. With the other hand, align the leader thread along the length of the bunch of fibre, overlapping by about 2 inches.

STEP 2 Allow twist to combine the leader thread and new fibres and create a strong join. This will require more twist than a long draw.

STEP 3 As the fibres join, fan out the fibre bunch between the fingers and thumb to separate and loosen the parallel fibres and allow the twist to take them into the thread. Both hands can be used, momentarily, to establish the fan shape if necessary.

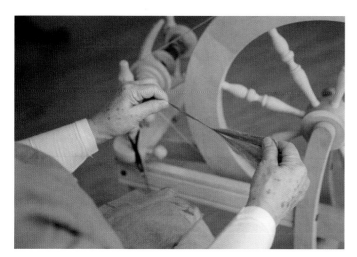

STEP 4 With the hand nearest the orifice, gently draw a few fibres forward towards the point of twist at the orifice to create a smooth, even yarn. Allow sufficient twist to enter the thread and then draw it out to the desired thickness between the two hands.

STEP 5 Allow the finished thread to be drawn onto the bobbin, smoothing it as it is drawn in.

SHORT FORWARD DRAW

The most commonly seen hand spinning technique is short forward draw. This yields a closely packed worsted-type yarn with which it is possible to achieve an exceptionally high degree of consistency. Only small quantities, 2 or 3 inches of thread, are made at a time and the fibre is under very controlled conditions. A high tension is used to draw thread out from the fibre hand as well as wind it onto the bobbin. Unfortunately, the tension on the wheel has a habit of creeping into the spinner unless deliberate action is taken to relax, sit back and avoid accepting the tension.

Fibre preparation for short draw can be anything from direct from a suitable fleece, from rovings, or carded tops through to rolags or punis (*see* Chapter 5).

SEMI-WORSTED DRAW

The semi-worsted technique is a method by which fibres are spun by folding them over the forefinger and drawing them forward onto the bobbin (spinning from half way along the staple, hence the term 'semi-worsted').

This is a very easy method to learn and useful for longer stapled fibre such as Suri alpaca or wool of 4-inch staple or more.

STEP-BY-STEP
SHORT FORWARD DRAW

STEP 1 Take a bunch of fibres, either straight from the fleece, roving, rolag or puni and lay the leader thread across them, overlapping by an inch or more. Draw out a few fibres from the fibre hand so that the fibres and leader are lying close together and the leader is still supported in the fibre hand.

STEP 2 Start the wheel, turning clockwise, with the hand nearest the orifice, and take hold of the leader thread. Feel the twist as it develops in the leader thread between finger and thumb and gently release the hold to allow twist into the fibre bunch and make a join.

STEP 3 When the join is established, draw a few more fibres from the fibre hand in towards the orifice, keeping hold of the leader thread and allow the twist in, as necessary, to maintain the join.

STEP 4 When 2 or 3 inches of thread are made, allow them through the orifice and onto the bobbin.

STEP 5 With the orifice hand, draw out 2 or 3 inches of fibre from that hand. Try to fan out the fibres smoothly as they are released from the fibre hand, as this will make drafting easier.

SEMI-WORSTED DRAW

STEP 1 The most difficult part is, in the first instance, joining onto the leader thread.

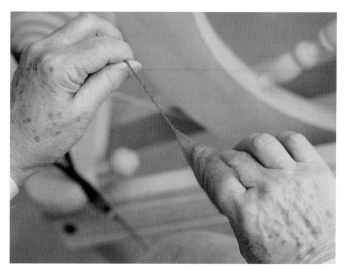

STEP 2 Drawing the thread. Semi-worsted draw can yield an exceptionally fine yarn and therefore requires a high degree of twist.

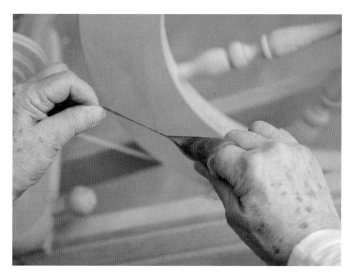

STEP 3 The draw can be made away from the wheel, as well as towards it, making it a very satisfying way to spin that yields a beautifully smooth, fine yarn – even from an inexperienced spinner.

CORE SPINNING

Core spun yarn is most often seen as bouclé, which consists of three elements: a core, a wrapping, and a binding thread. Core spinning is the first two of these elements, the core and a second fibre which is wrapped around it. The variations on a theme of core spinning are endless and it is the basis of many innovative and artistic hand-spun yarns. The core itself can be of commercial yarn as it seldom shows and it speeds up production; the wrapped fibre or thread provides the interest. Skill level for learning is relatively easy, 4 or 5 out of 10, and the rewards are quick and very striking. Lustrous long wools and rainbow dyed pre-drafted rovings make excellent wrapping fibre. When the two stages are completed, the core-spun yarn is unstable and behaves like a singles until it is either plied back again or stabilized by slightly felting or treating in some way such as with xanthan gum (*see* Chapters 6 and 9).

Learning to core spin is an invaluable skill and nowhere near as difficult as learning to spin in the first instance.

Working with loose fibres can become tiresome if they are continuously getting caught up on hooks, so a wheel with a large, or no, orifice, and sliding rings or large hooks, makes life easier. A jumbo flyer or wheel set to a low turning ratio will also allow more time for wrapping.

The wrapping fibres are best drafted in advance to avoid over-twisting. Long, lustrous fibres such as *mohair locks* are best separated out in advance. They make superb bouclé.

It makes sense to choose the core carefully, selecting colours that are

CORE SPINNING

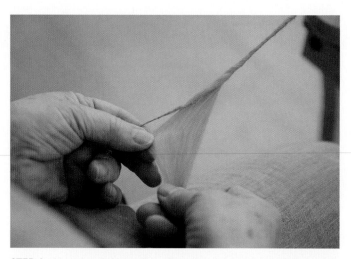

STEP 1 Place the core ball in a wool bowl on the floor to one side (say on the left for a right-handed spinner). This will stop it rolling about and attaching to rovings which are best kept in a basket on the other side.

STEP 2 Tie the Z (plied or singles) core thread to the leader and prepare to spin Z, turning the wheel in a clockwise direction, as for spinning singles. (If the core is S plied, then wrapping must be S direction otherwise the core will be seriously weakened or may even disintegrate.)

STEP 3 Keep the core under gentle tension between the third and fourth fingers of your left hand. This tension on the core is essential to ensure the rovings wrap around it.

STEP 4 Use your right hand to place the rovings alongside the core so that it attaches and wraps itself around the core. Aim to spread the wrapping area along the length of the core by working with both hands close together and separating the fibres along the core. Avoid holding the roving out at right angles to the core.

STEP 5 Working with hands side by side, and the thumb and forefinger of the left hand, it is possible to drag the fibre along the core to increase the width of take up while maintaining tension with the other fingers. If the wrap becomes too thin, then go back and apply more. This is the most difficult part of the technique and turning the wheel slowly or stopping it at times is helpful.

comfortable with each other. If the core and wrap colours are indistinguishable then mistakes, such as the core showing through, will not be so apparent. Also, a core yarn that is made from fluffy, woollen fibres will attach more easily to the wrapping fibre than a smooth acrylic or silk yarn.

Be careful with commercial yarns on the cone when core spinning: the action of taking the yarn off the cone creates unwanted twist so, to avoid this, wind the yarn off into balls or use a turntable.

The direction of twist in the core yarn is critical as applying the wrapping fibre effectively unwinds or over-twists the core. If the core is already plied, this is not such a serious issue as it will be unlikely to disintegrate. But, if the core is a Z-spun singles and the wrapping applied in S direction, the core will unwrap and the yarn will have no integrity. If the wrapping is applied in Z direction, then this will increase the twist in the core, making it stronger.

Regardless of whether the core is plied or single it will need to be rebalanced when the wrapping is complete as it will be unstable and behave like a singles. One way to do this is for the wrapped core spun thread to be plied again in the opposite direction with a binding thread, as in a classic bouclé (*see* Chapter 9).

The other, more complex, method is to take out twist as it is created. To do this, the core thread is wound onto a drop spindle, which is held loosely in one hand so that it can turn freely (in the opposite direction to the wheel) taking out the extra twist while you apply the

wrap with the other hand. This requires practice and a degree of dexterity, but it is easily learned (see Sarah Anderson's book, *The Spinner's Book of Yarn Designs*, page 194). For beginners, it is easier to make a classic three-stage bouclé and let the application of the final binding thread balance out the extra twist that was created when wrapping the core.

Core-spun yarns can be quite bulky but it is not necessary to spin 1,000 yards at a time. Just a few yards of carefully chosen coloured, fibrous or textural core-spun yarn can make a big statement in a piece of work. A little goes a long way.

Perhaps a purist would feel that using bought yarn in a hand-spun or crafted yarn is cheating. Right or wrong, it's your decision – it does not matter. Just learn a few basic skills and there is a whole new world of spinning techniques out there, just waiting to be explored.

Y SPIN Z?

Throughout this chapter, the wheel has, hopefully, been turning in a clockwise direction and outputting Z-spun yarn, or spinning Z twist.

It is vital that a spinner is able to recognize whether a thread is spun Z or S. If not, how does one know which way to ply it – or use it as a core? Turn the wheel the wrong way and thread disintegrates; ply two threads in the wrong direction and you create a mass of energized 'squirmals'.

A detailed explanation of the concept of S and Z is included in Chapter 6 but, briefly, the traditional method of identification is to look at the centre stem of the letters S and Z (S slants top left to bottom right; Z slants top right to bottom left) and interpret this into the yarn.

The key to identifying it in a singles thread yarn is to read it like a book: starting from the top left-hand side of the 'page', hold the yarn vertically and imagine it cut off at a point marking the top of the 'page'. At the very top left of the page, the fibre or thread will either be dangling down like a snake in a game of snakes and ladders, or it will not. If it is a snake, it is S spun. If the thread cannot be seen dangling down like a snake from the top left-hand side of the page, it must, therefore, be Z.

There are other methods, but for the meantime, just think: s*nakes are* not *for s*pinning.

Folding a singles thread in half on to itself will result in a 2-ply yarn made in the opposite direction to the twist. Hence, a single Z spun will ply itself in S direction.

IN A NUTSHELL

Different spinning techniques, such as worsted, woollen and core spun, have a major influence on the texture, performance and appearance of hand-spun yarn – others include fibre, colour and yarn structure. Mastering these basic spinning techniques is the primary, and most demanding, challenge in becoming a hand spinner.

4 Sheep Fleece: Nature's Best

Spinning time is quality time and too precious to waste on unsuitable fleece, fibre or equipment. The objective of this chapter is to show how to recognize the easiest fleece to spin in its raw state, and save pain, strain and disappointment.

At the present time, wool is our most undervalued and wasted resource. It is 100 percent natural, renewable, sustainable and biodegradable, as well as the most fire resistant of all commonly used fibres. The Campaign for Wool, whose Patron is HRH Prince of Wales, is working to promote wool and the many ways in which it can be used to benefit the community and environment. As a result, wool is now being actively promoted by leading design professionals and fashion houses.

It is no accident that sheep have been domesticated for thousands of years, as there is nothing equal to wool for hand spinning. Wool has resilience, elasticity and takes dye easily. It traps air and it can absorb nearly a third of its weight in water without feeling wet. Sheep are fairly easily managed, and their fleece a naturally renewable resource.

Primitive breeds of sheep such as Soay have an undercoat of wool, supplemented by coarse hairs, kemp, which are released into the wool for added protection in winter.

Wool grows in clumps or locks of fibre. At a microscopic level, each fibre is a single or double cortex surrounded by a 'skin' of overlapping scales. The scales overlap, pointing towards the growth tip of the fibre – away from the skin. The more scales there are, the more coarse the fleece will feel.

SPINNING 'IN THE GREASE'

Imagine a warm June day: shearers are leaning over sheep that sit on their bottoms, bellies splayed out like bags of water as the clippers, driven by noisy Lister engines, leave the sheep clean and fresh. Those catching the sheep, shearing them, and rolling the wool, may sweat and strain. But to a hand spinner, spinning 'in the grease' is literally no sweat!

Fleece can come off like a giant marshmallow, all fluffy and warm, or like a blanket in one sad lump. The marshmallows are the ones to spin in the grease – spinning bliss! The wool nearly spins itself: just attach a few fibres and the spinning wheel does the rest.

Sadly, few spinners get the chance to spin a fleece as it comes off the sheep. But fleece is becoming more readily available, as increasing numbers of people are able to keep small flocks and want to see their produce put to good use. Spinners need to know how to find their way about a fleece and how to pick the best for hand spinning. And remember that a raw fleece that is warm is easier to spin.

When a fleece is rolled in the traditional manner the best quality fibre is on the outside where it can be seen. When the shearer has finished, the fleece is gathered up and thrown out onto a board or smooth surface free from straw and dirt; it is thrown so that the cut side lands downwards and fibre tips uppermost. Any dirty 'daggings' from the tail end are pulled off and discarded as far as the spinner is concerned. The sides are folded in towards the middle overlapping by about two thirds.

Then, starting at the tail end, the fleece is rolled up towards the neck end, making a firm roll. Some of the neck end fleece is then twisted into a rope and wrapped around the roll of fleece and tucked in.

A well rolled fleece appears neat and clean, it can be handled without falling apart and, most importantly from a sales perspective, it looks its best. The finest quality fleece is presented on the outside of the bundle where it is handled and the clean, sunny, cut side is all that shows. Inside the parcel could be a different story!

Never, under any circumstances, buy a fleece without unwrapping and carefully assessing it for its suitability for hand spinning. There is much to consider, and it requires many of our senses: sight, feel, smell, hearing and the most important of all, common sense.

Fleece 'in the grease'.

It makes sense to get as much information as possible about the sheep when
buying fleece. How old is it? Has it been
well fed and cared for? When was it shorn
(no-one wants last year's leftovers)? Is it
from a ewe or a ram? How is the fleece
presented – is it rolled in the traditional
manner or stuffed haphazardly in an
old feed bag with other fleece? Is the
breeder's contact information attached?
It is common sense do a bit of simple
research through the vendor before
even bothering to examine the fleece.
Remember the vendor's agenda is to sell;
your agenda is pleasure. Take time to
examine the fleece very carefully. It takes many, many hours to get from fleece to yarn
and the process should be a pleasure, not a pain. You don't want to learn what 'getting
fleeced' feels like!

Fleece with a break in the staple is not
suitable for hand spinning.

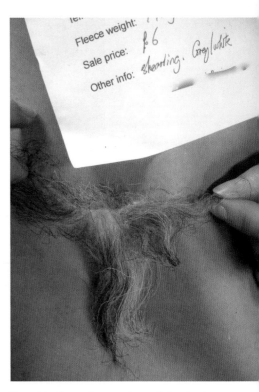

Shearling fleece frequently contains short
lamb wool fibres which cause pilling.

STAPLE

As the fleece grows on the sheep it forms
itself into little bunches, known as locks
or staples, which adhere together at the
end of the growth, forming a tip. As the
tip ends become subject to weather and
friction they tend to be a different colour
from the clean new growth at the skin.
When the fleece is shorn, the length of
staple (the distance from the tip to the cut
end) varies from breed to breed. Staple
length can be anything from 1 inch, in a
Manx Loaghtan, for example, to 15 inches
in a Leicester Longwool breed. Lambs
are not normally shorn in the first year
of their life.

Shearlings are sheep being shorn for
the first time at over a year old. As the
lamb grows its adult wool it doesn't necessarily shed its lamb wool and this can
be seen either at the base of the staple,
or adhering to the tips looking like curly
ends. Thus the staple length may appear
longer than it actually is. There may also
be a mix of short and long fibres within
the staple.

Firstly, it is common sense to choose
a breed, and hence a fleece, that fits
the purpose. For beginners a staple
length between 3 and 5 inches is easiest to manage. Breeds such as the Jacob,
Shetland, Blue-faced Leicester and
crossbreeds with a 3–5 inch staple are
a good choice for both beginners and
most hand-spun projects. Such fleece
yields a soft, warm, lofty yarn ideal for
knitting and crochet.

The long wool breeds – Wensleydale,
Leicester Longwool, Gotland, etc. – have
a lustrous appearance and staple can be
anything from a handspan up to 15 inches
long. These breeds yield a more solid,
strong thread suitable for weaving or
dyeing. When skilfully spun, these make
intensely beautiful, lustrous yarn that
takes colour and refracts light.

Generally the primitive breeds, such
as Soay, or hill breeds, such as Herdwick,
are more coarse and therefore ideal for
rugs and upholstery.

COMPARE AND CONTRAST

The best quality fibre within each fleece
is from the shoulders and neck area; the
poorest from the back end, legs and belly.
In some fleece the difference is insignificant, but it is important to compare by
taking a lock from each place. Firstly take
a sample of the best quality lock, which
should pull out easily; is each fibre fine,
straight or wavy? If it is wavy then this will
facilitate a lofty yarn as the crimp will trap
air. If the fibre is straight then it will make
a smooth, more solid yarn depending on
the spinning technique employed.

Now hold the lock up to the light. Are
there any breaks in the fibre? Give it a tug
with both hands to see if it has integrity.
If it breaks, discard the whole fleece. Are
there areas of density visible against the
light? If so, hold the tip and pull through

a hand carder. This will indicate how much short fibre or waste there will be – and how much work will be needed to remove it.

Now take the poorer quality sample and examine the fineness or otherwise of the fibre. Look for kemp, coarse white hair-like fibres that are released in the fleece in the winter for added protection from the weather. Kemp is easy to identify as it is pointed at both ends. Kemp will need to be removed; it is more common in primitive breeds with coarser fleece and mostly found around the back legs or britch area of the fleece.

Comparing the two locks will show up how much difference there is between the fine and coarse fibres. The greater the difference between the two samples, the greater will be the waste. In some fleece there is little difference, but the degree of difference varies within the breed, flock, and from sheep to sheep.

USE YOUR SENSES

See it

Bearing in mind the information gleaned about the fleece, begin with what the eye can see. Does the information you've been given tie in with what you can see? For example, if you are told this is a long wool fleece and the staple is only 3 inches long, ask yourself why. Has it been shorn once this year already? Is this fleece from a sheep being shorn for the first time? If so, it is likely to have the lamb wool and new growth either at the base or tips of the staple.

First shearing, contrary to popular belief, requires a lot of extra work in order to yield a top quality yarn. Did the ewe have lambs this year? If not, the fleece might be very good quality as the ewe's

Nature provides some lovely colours.

constitution was not depleted by breeding. Conversely, if the sheep did not 'winter well' its fleece will reflect this. Just think of a 'bad hair day'!

Assuming the fleece is rolled in the traditional manner, open it up by untucking the neck roll. (If it isn't wrapped, why are you bothering with something no-one else bothered with?) Carefully unwrap the fleece and lay it out on a sheet or somewhere where it will not pick up foreign matter such as leaves or straw. Look for contaminants such as moss, seeds, grass, straw, burrs or thorns, which will take a lot of time and effort to remove.

Pay particular attention to the tail end, as, unpleasant as this may be, fleece can become infested, and spinners need to know about this. Flies lay eggs at the sheep's tail, the eggs turn into maggots, and these feed on live flesh as part of their natural life cycle. It is rare to find maggots and larvae, but it can happen.

On a more agreeable note, colour is great joy in spinning, and nature provides a wonderful selection which never fails to sit comfortably with itself. Much fleece is a creamy white and easy to see when spinning on dark winter days.

The range of natural fleece colours is so wide that it might be worth asking yourself, is the natural colour pleasing, and is it likely to remain so after several weeks' preparing and spinning it? Does the colour remind you of a good time or place? Does it inspire an end project? There is always the option of dye – see Chapter 8.

At this stage, take note of any foreign colours in the raw fleece, such as red or blue used for identifying sheep. This is usually raddle, a waxy crayon-like substance used to identify mated ewes in the breeding season; although it is supposed to be washable, washing out raddle requires extra work so is something to be aware of, but may not be reason to decline the fleece altogether.

Feel it

No-one is going to take a microscope to measure the fineness of a fibre. Nor is it necessary. A fine fibre will feel softer in the hand than a coarse one. If there is doubt, stroke the fibres across your cheek where the skin is more sensitive. Handling and stroking fibres across your face at the same time will reveal as much as is necessary to know which to choose for hand spinning. Run your hands lightly over the whole fleece to see if there are any thistles; these are always easier to feel than spot, and they spoil the spinning experience!

Smell it

Among its many desirable characteristics – wool is soft, warm, breathable, natural, fire-retardant, bio-degradable, recyclable – there is that lovely enduring woolly smell. This contrasts strongly with the smell from some sheep (particularly rams) which is enduring, but not endearing. All fleece has a smell which most people do not find in the least bit disagreeable. In fact, to many people it reminds them of home, and most spinners love it. However, for the purposes of critical assessment, take a good sniff, and try to be impartial: if you have the least dislike or doubt about the smell, then do not consider spinning it. If it smells now – presumably out of doors – imagine what it will be like when it reaches 21°C in the sitting room next winter.

Remember also that smell is subjective, so those who share your living space may not find it tolerable even if you do. Worse still, a smell can remain in the fibre no matter how much washing and scouring is done. Washed as fleece, washed again as yarn, washed again as the finished item, the ram smell can resist all efforts to eradicate it. Worse still, it even seems to have the power of reincarnation! The smell can come back again after it has been washed and stored away. So do not ignore the smelly warning signals at this stage.

It is no pleasure to spend a winter spinning and knitting a pullover only to find you smell like an old sheep wearing it.

Hear it

Strange as it may seem, a sound fleece will sound it. Take the two sample locks as explained earlier. Hold each, one at a time, between your two hands and 'twang' them with a short, sharp snatch somewhere near your ear. If it twangs a note, that is a good sign. If it sounds like a dull thud, or worse still breaks, then the fibre has some sort of fault and will not make a quality yarn. Sometimes the fault can be due to a change in diet, adverse weather, poor health, just as human hair will reveal health history in the laboratory. But you don't need to get scientific about it, as a short, sharp twang will reveal all.

If in doubt…

…leave it out. There is more fleece in the world at this very moment than spinners will ever spin. And a new crop comes every year. Ask any spinner and they will admit to having a fleece, or two or more, that they doubt will ever get spun because… you only need to look at the above paragraphs to find a few of the likely reasons.

Be discerning. Even if it is free, a fleece won't necessarily merit your free time. Fleece is plentiful and, unless it is very special, cheap. For the cost of a 100gm ball of commercially produced yarn a spinner can buy a fine quality fleece weighing ten times this much.

Knowing how to choose fleece for hand spinning is predominantly about knowing what to avoid. This is frequently not because the fleece is poor quality but because preparing it for handspinning will take up an inordinate and unnecessary amount of time; time that could be mindfully spent behind the spinning wheel creating beautiful yarn and engaged in something that puts meaning into life.

Learning to spin deserves the best fibre, the best wheels, the best teachers, and beginners can only discover this by a process of elimination. Being critical about fleece will shorten the learning curve to the place where life is good, and spinning is joy.

For further information on which breeds to choose for a particular yarn or project, see *Pure Wool: A Knitter's Guide to Using Single-breed Yarns* by Sue Blacker.

WASHING AND PREPARATION

CLEANING THE FLEECE

Whether to spin 'in the grease' or wash fleece first is a matter of personal preference. There is a body of opinion that suggests spinning in the grease spins dirt in, making it difficult to wash the dirt out.

There is an equally valid point of view that in washing and carding fleece it loses its natural character, rather like over-processed food loses its taste. If it is to be spun in the grease then the choice of fleece will be for an open texture, with locks that separate easily. It will preferably be clean with no foreign bodies and not require carding unless one is prepared to accept that the carding equipment will also become 'in the grease'.

There are dozens of different ways to wash fleece: a big overnight cold soak, by the sink-load, in the washing machine on the wool programme, in really hot water, in cold water, washing with liquid wool wash, biological washing liquid, soap flakes, washing up liquid, vinegar…. You can even tie it in a horse's hay net and dunk it in the river – if there is a river nearby with open access. (This is an interesting method as you can see the grease permeating the water around it). All methods work; it is simply a question of personal choice.

However, if you are after the best results with minimum effort, then washing by hand in the kitchen sink is as good a way as any. No special equipment is necessary and there is no heavy lifting involved. To do this, fill the sink with hand-hot water. It is not essential to add cleaning agent as the wool contains its own, but this is a matter of preference. Gently immerse a smallish quantity – say, 300g – and leave it to soak for an hour or two. By this time the water will be nearly cold and the fleece can be agitated to clean any difficult bits and is unlikely to felt in the cooler water.

Wool will turn to felt if subjected to heat and friction at the same time. Felting takes place when the microscopic scales that make up a wool fibre open up and lock into each other – rather like the fingers and thumbs of your two hands can lock together – and nothing will take them apart. Taking note of the current temperature, remove fleece from the water, and rinse it in water of the same temperature. Fabric softener does not work with wool so is not necessary unless for its residual scent. When rinsed clean,

wring out with your hands and dry out of doors on a bench, or sheet. It is best to avoid direct sunlight as this can also cause felting.

The ideal time to wash wool is in the summer, as soon after shearing as possible. The grease and dirt seems to be easier to remove at the early stage. Shearing takes place in early summer, which is conveniently followed by plenty of opportunities for wool washing on good drying days throughout the summer months. When clean and dry the wool can be stored in hessian sacks. If it is stored indoors for a long period it will become very dry due to the home atmosphere and may need to be sprayed with water from a hand held plant-type sprayer before spinning. Very dry wool is brittle and difficult to spin.

TEASING AND CARDING

Some fleece can be spun straight from the lock or at the very least simply teased out by hand prior to spinning. To do this take a single lock, which is easily identifiable by the different coloured tip, and tease it out by hand until the individual fibres are loosely held together. Any foreign bodies can be picked out at the same time.

If the wool contains lots of short fibres or foreign bodies these can be removed by taking each lock in turn. Take a firm hold of one end of the lock and pull it through a carder. This will open up the fibres to make a fluffy fibre bunch; now take hold of the other end and pull that through so that all fibres are separated out throughout the lock. It is more practical to take the time to clean a whole basket of fleece rather than card and spin one lock at a time.

There are three types of carder suitable for this process: the flick carder, hand

carders, and the table carder. There is also a mechanical drum carder which does not clean fibre but is used for separating and blending, and also a blending board. Other specialized products and equipment for wool preparation include the picker, wool combs and hackles. Such devices involve sharp teeth and risk!

For the gentle art of hand spinning it is rarely necessary to resort to such forceful and extreme measures to prepare fleece. If it is thought necessary to use force in fleece preparation then it might be wise to ask a few fundamental questions, such as, should I be spinning this fleece? Is this the best use of my time? Will this bring me joy? Spinning is quality time, and merits quality fibre. Here, we discuss in detail only the most commonly used equipment and ethically sourced fibre.

Flick carder
A flick carder is the simple brush-like tool suitable for use with fleece that contains very few short fibres and very little foreign matter. It is used with a suede leather pad or leather apron on the knee. Take a lock and hold it firmly by one end, resting your hand on the leather pad, and with the carder, flick, tease or just comb out the fibres until they are open and fluffy. Turn the lock around and repeat. All the fibres will be facing the same direction and it is preferable to store them in this order for ease of spinning.

Hand carders
Hand carders are larger than the flick carder and come in pairs. They are sold according to the number of pins per inch in the carding area. The number of pins per square inch (ppi) varies: 36, 72, 108, 120. As the number of pins per square inch increases the individual pins become finer and, usually, more flexible.

Curved carders with long, flexible pins are ideal for making rolags.

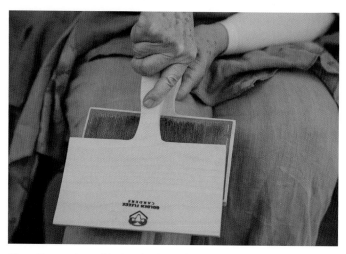

Clean the carders with the pins in perfect alignment.

Obviously the finer the ppi, the finer will be the cleaning and separating effect on the fibres. 120ppi carders will card fine fibre such as alpaca or angora, whereas with a lower ppi fine fibre simply floats across the thicker, less densely packed pins. Carders can either be flat or curved, and the handles can either be attached to the back or the edge of the carder. The most versatile carders are lightweight and curved with integral handles and lots of long, flexible pins, the reasons for which are explained below.

Hand carders are used in three different ways. A single carder is used for cleaning fleece and is ideal for combing out short fibres and debris from medium length staples. Hold the carder in the left hand (or the right if you are left handed); grasp it firmly with the palm downwards as palm upwards puts undue strain on the wrist. At the same time rest the carder on the lap or a table top and, while holding it firmly in place pull a lock firmly through the pins with the right hand. This will take out any debris, leaving one end of the fibres clean and separated out. Now turn the fibres around and pull the other end through.

Debris is removed from cleaned carders.

As the debris builds up in the left-hand carder it will need to be cleaned out. To do this hold the carder against your leg with the left hand, handle pointing upwards. With the other carder, also handle upwards, put the two together, one directly on top of the other so that the pins are touching. Now carefully move the carders up and down against each other keeping them close together and aligned so that the pins can pass other.

The carder pins are correlated and perfect alignment is required in order for the carders to pass over each other; this can be felt rather than achieved by sight. The movement forces the rubbish into a roll at the handle edge of the carders where it can be picked off and discarded, leaving the carders clean.

The hand carders can also be used together for carding and separating fibres. But this will not remove debris. Hold carders as you would hold a table tennis bat – by the handle with the effective part in front of your hand where it can be manipulated easily and speedily in free flowing movements.

CARDING

STEP 1   To card, first load the left (or right if preferred) carder, placed so that the handle is facing outwards; load two or three locks of fibre tips or base towards the handle onto the carder. (It is possible to overload the carder, but not under-load it. If you are unsure, load less, not more.)

STEP 2   Next, grasp the other carder in the right hand, place it directly above the loaded carder and *very gently* comb away (as gently as if combing someone's hair). Any pressure will force the fibre down into the pins from whence it will not card, making it extremely hard work. It may be necessary to comb two or three times, seldom more.

STEP 3   Now strip the right-hand card by placing the tip against the base of the left one so that the fibres just begin to grip and *lift* them off with the left carder.

STEP 4   Place the carder back on your knee or the table and using the empty right carder, card again three times.

STEP 5   Now strip off the left carder by placing the tip of it against the base of the right carder, and lift off with the right-hand carder. Card again until there is fibre on both carders.

STEP 6   The fibres can now be stripped off both carders in one movement. Place right carder tip to base of left, lift with left. Left carder tip is now at base of right, ready to lift fibre off all in the one movement. All fibres will now be floating lightly on the carder and lying parallel to each other ready for spinning worsted or woollen draw. Alternatively they can be rolled into rolags for woollen yarn.

ROLAGS

Rolags are a joy to spin and it is very easy to make sixty rolags per hour, which equates to very much more than an hour's delightful spinning time. What's more, the quality of a yarn reflects the amount of preparation that goes into it. A yarn spun from rolags made from combed fleece is consistently even with lots of loft and spring. This does not mean that yarn spun in the grease is inferior quality: a quality yarn is one that is fit for the purpose. It is quite unnecessary to make rolags for a thick pullover that will only ever be worn outdoors for gardening, driving or shepherding sheep. But if the pullover is to be worn in social situations, where it will be closely seen – and hopefully admired – then careful preparation of fleece and rolags will pay dividends.

MAKING ROLAGS

STEP 1   To make a rolag, take the fibres at the stage where they are floating lightly on the right-hand carder and lying parallel to each other.

STEP 2   Take up a few loose fibres from the outer edge and press them into the start of a roll.

STEP 3 Do not press carders close together when rolling rolags.

STEP 4 Lightly rolled rolags incorporate more air.

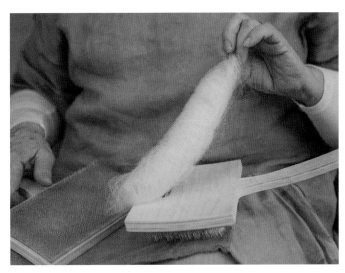

STEP 5 A rolag weighs as little as 1g.

PUNIS

In order to spin cotton and very short staple fibres it is necessary to card them as above but, instead of stripping the fibres off with the other carder, the fibre is carefully removed by wrapping it around a dowel about the size of a large pencil, lifting and dragging to pull the fibres closely round the dowel. This creates a solid roll of fibre known as a puni. Cotton is rarely hand spun at the present time; however, the technique has been adapted for dyed wool to great popularity and effect.

A puni is quite different from a rolag in its structure, use and origin. The term 'puni' originates in the tradition of cotton spinning, and 'rolag' derives from wool spinning. Whereas a rolag is extremely light (weighing as little as 1g), and about an inch or two in diameter, a puni is much heavier (about 8g) and denser – a fairly solid roll of fibres about an inch in diameter, depending upon the diameter of the dowel. The length of the puni is determined by the width of the carders or blending board on which it is made.

A rolag could be described as a roll of air; a puni a roll of fibre. In spite of much confusion and possibly misunderstanding amongst equipment manufacturers, the puni and the rolag are two quite different entities in hand spinning.

Both rolags and punis are a delight to spin with, and the time taken in preparing them is richly rewarded in terms of spinning pleasure and purity of blending colours and natural fibres. In recent times the puni is mostly usually seen as a woollen, rather than a cotton preparation.

A puni is a very attractive way of presenting coloured fibre, and an even more interesting way of blending textures and different fibres, particularly those that refract light. They are very easy to spin and can also be felted for jewellery or tapestry inlay.

Blending board

Today's attractive punis are made on flat blending boards using gloriously coloured wool and luxury fibres, sometimes including light refracting Angelina or lustrous silk rovings and longwools. They are particularly attractive when coiled and rolled and are very easy to spin, especially for beginners. Even without being spun at all they can be used to add colour and texture in woven and felted textile work. Before the advent of blending boards in 2013 the puni was seldom used creatively and its use for making designer yarns is relatively unexplored. Lots of new opportunities exist here for yarns with innovative structures of lightly spun fibres that have both novelty, integrity and ingenuity.

Blending boards are usually rectangular, measuring 12–18 inches (30–45cm) and are used with a brush, similar in size to a flick carder. They may have a rubber backing or removable keel attached to the back to avoid slippage in use. Boards vary in pin densities, usually from 72ppi to 120ppi, and are supplied with two dowels. Beginners may find it is easier to use three dowels for rolling the puni.

The process begins with applying different coloured or textured fibre to the board in even layers. If filling the whole board it is better to start the first layer half way down filling the bottom half and then start at the top to apply the remainder. It is important to spread fibre evenly and not leave any thin patches.

In a puni, combed fibre is tightly rolled around dowel(s).

Punis are attractive and easy to spin.

STEP-BY-STEP
MAKING PUNIS

STEP 1 Layers of fibre are brushed onto the blending board, starting from the top of the board and working towards the bottom. Around 40–50g of fibre can be applied to the board.
(Puni by J. Goodey.)

STEP 2 To roll the puni, start at the bottom and using the brush, lift the first few fibres away from the pins. Place one dowel underneath the layer of fibre, and one on top so that the fibre is trapped between the two dowels.

STEP 3 Using both hands grip either end of the two dowels firmly and turn them over together so that the fibres are securely wrapped around both dowels. (Some people find that adding a third dowel at this stage makes it easier to remove the puni later on.) Gently ease the fibres up off the pins to make combing and rolling easier.

STEP 4 Next, lift the dowels slightly away from the board and pull them towards you, drawing out the fibres to form a smooth layer. Now roll the fibre layer around the dowels.

STEP 5 Repeat the process until you have about a third of the board on the dowels. To complete the puni draw it away from the remaining fibre on the board. Smooth any loose fibres into place with your hands as if you were polishing it. The large Golden Fleece blending board shown here accommodates enough fibre to make several punis.

STEP 6 Slightly off-setting the dowels also makes it easier to pull them apart when it comes to removing the finished puni. To take the puni off the dowels, carefully slide the dowels out one at a time. Should the dowels become stuck – hence reason for offsetting – place one vertically on a solid edge and press down the other using the handle of the small blending brush. Aim to make three punis per full board, each weighing about 10–15g. The above method is a guideline only and can be adapted as necessary.

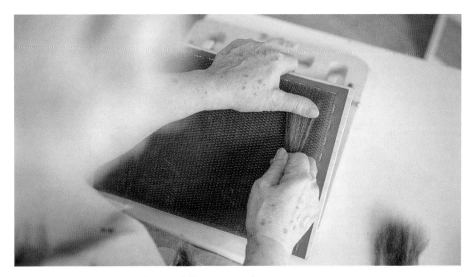

A table carder takes the strain out of fibre preparation.

TABLE CARDER

For long stapled fleece or one that contains short fibres or debris, the table carder is by far the easiest and best option for cleaning, combing and preparing fleece for spinning. It has strong, short pins and the device is clamped securely to a table, leaving both hands free to pull out and comb the locks of fleece through the carder.

Repetitively pulling any quantity of fleece through a small hand carder is tedious and places great strain on the hands, arms and shoulders. The table carder takes the strain out of the task and gives much better results due to its size and stability. The generous width allows for longer stapled locks of fleece or fibre, such as Suri alpaca, to be combed several times at different places across the carder each time. In this way it is easy to see when the lock is clean and the unwanted short fibres and debris build up more on one side making it easier to see when the lock is clean.

DRUM CARDER

Drum carders are dual-purpose carding devices used for separating fibres and blending different fibres and colours in bulk quantities. It is important to be clear that this is the purpose of a drum carder: it will not clean or remove debris from fleece. If a patch of debris such as straw or dead leaves is drum carded in with

the fleece all that will happen is that the debris will be spread over a wider area of fleece than before. The debris is also now in smaller pieces, making it even more difficult to remove than ever.

In fibre preparation the drum carder will separate fibres, aligning them parallel to each other ready for spinning. A batt, the output of the drum carder, is a batch of carded fibres that can be drawn out to make rovings or laid over other batts and fed through the carder again for further mixing or blending. For large quantities of fibre that need processing the drum carder saves hours of physical effort. Batts can also be rolled in short lengths to make rolag-like bundles for spinning. They can also be stored without deterioration, unlike rolags which squash very easily.

The drum carder is excellent for blending colours and creating batts of different fibres which can be carded several times for effect. It comprises two drums, one large with strong pins and the other a small drum that takes up the fibre and

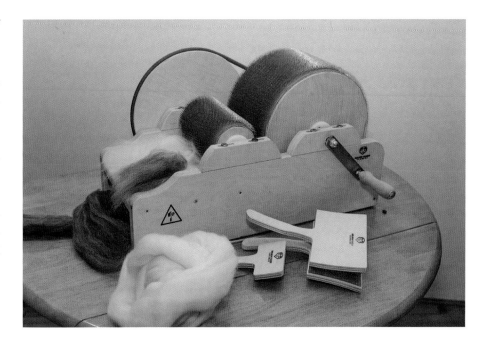

Hand spun – for life! Centre: grey pullover (breed unknown) spun in 1989 from carded fleece with all short fibres removed, worn for 20 years without pilling. Left: Manx Loaghtan pullover, 2008. Spun straight from the fleece with the sun-bleached tips of the locks of fibre left intact to preserve the appearance of the breed in the yarn. Right: Hebridean sleeveless pullover, 2010.

feeds it onto the large drum. The teeth of both should be adjusted to be as close as possible without touching. If the teeth touch there is an unpleasant scratching sound. Fibre needs to be fed into the smaller, licker-in drum a little at a time, separated into small locks. If any pressure is put on the fibre as it is fed in, then the fibre will wrap around the licker-in drum. So feed in the separated locks by dropping them on the feed-in area and gently push forwards avoiding any backwards pressure.

The newest carders include a packer brush which embeds the fibres into the large drum creating batts of up to 70g of fibre on a standard 8-inch width device. Like hand carders, the drum carders come in coarse, medium or fine pins and as the number of pins per inch increases, the pins themselves are finer and more flexible. Drum carders come in different widths and are normally turned by hand. The batts are removed after releasing the packer brush with a doffer stick. Starting at the furthermost edge where the card-ing cloth meets there is a ridge to prevent damaging the cloth with the doffer. Lift and separate an inch or so of fibre at a time with the doffer until the whole batt can be lifted off a little at a time, turning the drum as necessary.

PILLING

Pilling, those annoying small bobbles of fibre that appear on knitwear, is such a common problem that there are many products on the market specifically for shaving or removing the pills. Pilling is a result of short fibres in the yarn working their way to the surface during wear. To avoid the problem it is essential to remove short fibres, frequently lamb wool, from fleece prior to spinning it. This involves a lot of additional work in fleece preparation and is a good reason to be circumspect when choosing fleece.

No amount of hand or drum carding will prevent pilling. The only way to avoid pilling is to remove short fibres in the first instance and avoid spinning short and long fibres together in the same yarn. Short fibres need to be removed at the outset. Otherwise once blended and spun in, short fibres simply work their way back out again. The table carder makes this easy, but it can also

be done using hand carders. The grey pullover pictured was spun in 1989 and has worn every winter since. There are signs of wear at the neck as one would expect, and the whole thing has taken on the shape of the wearer. But notice there is no pilling – even after 26 years. All the short fibres were painstakingly removed from the fleece using hand carders and only long fibres were made into rolags prior to spinning.

Twenty-five years is not an unrealistic lifetime of wear for a quality handspun pullover. Such garments do not need washing after every wear, but do need to be stored clean. The most common problem is damage by moths. Happily, for hand spinners at least, moths always prefer fine quality fibres such as cashmere to the common sheep fleece breeds

beloved by most hand spinners. Time spent is preparation is minuscule when compared to the life-time of wear one can expect from a garment.

IN A NUTSHELL

There is huge pleasure in handling fleece, particularly if you know where it comes from, or who you are spinning it for – even if it is yourself! It is an act of love. Time spent in preparation is all part of the joy of being a hand spinner, along with the knitting or weaving. Spinning time is too valuable to be wasted on poor quality fleece that can only ever yield poor quality yarn. Good spinners deserve good fleece.

5 Fibres for Hand Spinning

Wool is the most versatile, adaptable, accessible, high-performance fibre on the planet; the everyday substance of a spinner's life. Once you have become competent with wool, it is natural to want to try out your new-found skills on some of the more unusual and exotic fibres available, particularly if they are considered luxurious, or come from faraway places with strange-sounding names. But, like a holiday, exotic fibre is more the exception than the norm. The cost needs to be calculated in terms of ethics, and balanced against the fact that all fibre has a part to play in the creative process of spinning.

To be comfortable, spinners need to know – as far as it is ever possible to do so – that the fibre they are working with is as wholesome and environmentally friendly as the craft of spinning itself.

ANIMAL FIBRES: PROTEINS

There is a growing interest in other natural protein fibres such as those from alpaca, llama, goats, camel and rabbits, and the number of animals and fibres is increasing all the time. Unlike sheep, camelids, goats and rabbits all require skilled management and resources in order to thrive in temperate climates and yield their luxurious fibre, hair and fur. Many grow two types of hair: a soft undercoat which is the sought-after luxury fibre, along with a strong, wiry, guard hair, which prevents the soft warm fleece from matting and offers increased protection from the weather.

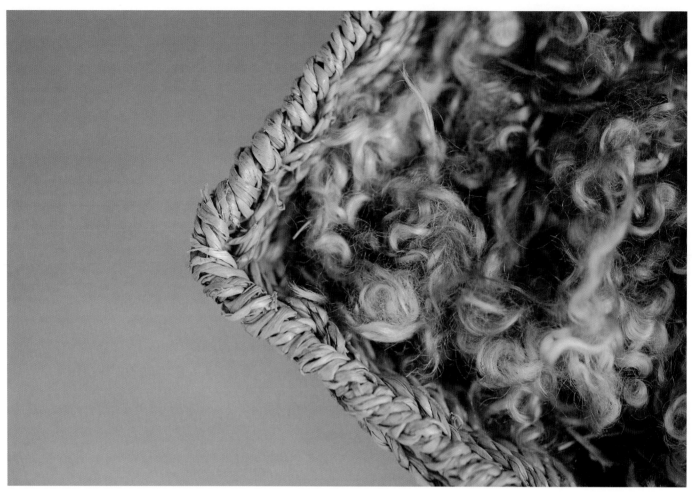

Hand-dyed mohair locks.

Angora goats have very little guard hair and lots of warm undercoat; conversely, cashmere goats have lots of guard hair and very little undercoat. Confusingly, Angora goats do not yield angora fibre: they yield mohair. Angora rabbits yield angora. Cashmere goats yield cashmere, but only about a quarter of the coat is any use for spinning.

ANGORA, MOHAIR AND CASHMERE

Angora goats (mohair)

The fibre from domesticated Angora goats is known as mohair. This is easily confused with angora fibre, which comes from Angora rabbits and is a totally different product.

Mohair from the Angora goat is naturally wavy, soft and silky and takes dye easily. Mohair feels smoother and is less likely to felt than wool because it has fewer scales on the cortex of the fibre. The staple length is 4–6 inches if the goats are shorn twice a year. It is stronger than most sheep's wool, although about the same fibre thickness, 25–40 microns. (A micron is one thousandth of a millimeter. As a comparison, human hair has a thickness of 40–50 microns.)

Angora goats yield their finest quality fibre (25 microns) over their first three shearings and, after this, the fibre gradually becomes more coarse. Angora goats yield 3–5 kg of usable fibre a year.

Cashmere goats

Cashmere goats have lots of guard hair and only about 25 percent of the total fleece is the much-prized undercoat.

Cashmere fibre is an extremely fine (<18 microns), luxurious fibre which is warm, lightweight and drapes beautifully. The cashmere undercoat has to be separated out from the guard hair very carefully and this is a costly and painstaking process requiring many man-hours. The staple length of cashmere is less than 2 inches and the yield is less than 150g per head per year.

Angora rabbit

Angora is a lightweight, hollow fur obtained from the domesticated angora rabbit. It felts very easily and is usually blended with other fibres where it imparts warmth and texture. Angora is very fine (only 10–15 microns) and fibre is either plucked or shorn. The Angora rabbit yields around 400g of fibre per year.

Animal welfare is a major concern and rabbits need to be kept very clean and require regular combing to keep their coats in top condition. There are serious ethical concerns about the welfare of these animals, particularly in the Far East, so sourcing of this fibre should be carefully considered.

ALPACA

Alpaca is soft, light, warm and non-allergenic. It feels smooth and a little slippery because it has a hollow fibre structure with fewer scales than wool. It comes in a pleasing range of colours, from white, greys, fawns, browns through to black. The fibre has no grease in it, but it can be dirty and dusty. A spinner who is not comfortable with the greasy feel of sheep wool would probably be very happy with alpaca.

Huacaya alpaca

There are two types of alpaca, the most common being Huacaya, which accounts for about 90 percent of the alpaca population.

The quality of Huacaya fibre varies widely, as does the amount of crimp and thickness of fibre, which can be from 14 up to 30 microns.

Huacaya fibre is often 3–5 inches in staple length and can have a crimp and elasticity, but little natural loft or spring. It is versatile and can be spun in different ways to counter its lack of loft. Spun worsted or semi-worsted it can make ultra fine lace weight shawls which drape well. On the other hand, alpaca spun using a woollen long draw will yield a lofty bulky fibre that is light, warm and suitable for knitted garments or projects. It seems to prefer to drape when knitted rather than spring or bounce like wool.

Suri alpaca

The less common Suri alpaca can be recognized by their straight, smooth, frequently long, and lustrous coats. Suri fibre is generally finer than Huacaya (10–14 microns) and its long staple is ideal for spinning worsted draw. Take small bunches of combed fibre, all lying in the same direction and fan them out to allow just a few to be taken up to form the finest of threads.

Suri alpaca is a very easy and pleasing fibre to spin. It benefits from being pulled through a table carder as the length of staple makes it unwieldy when using hand carders.

SILK

Silk is a glorious and unique textile, being the secretion of a moth. Silk production (sericulture), like spinning, has a fascinating history spanning thousands of years.

Silk comes in many forms, and is a joy to spin and wear. It has an affinity with colour and will take dye more easily and readily than any other fibre. It is astonishingly strong, feels warm to the touch and has a natural lustre that looks very good too. Unlike wool, silk will not felt or pill, but can be used with great effect in felting.

Silk is mainly sourced from the mulberry silk worm. Silk is extracted by unwinding the continuous filament that makes up the silk worm cocoon. It is the only natural filament used in textiles. Each thread can be over a thousand yards long and these lengths are selected for high quality commercial production. When threads break, or moths hatch, leaving holes in the cocoons, the resulting filaments are much shorter and these are ideal for hand spinning.

The shorter lengths, which are still very much longer than any other animal fibre staple, are made into handkerchief-sized squares called 'hankies', 'conical caps', and 'tops' for use in hand spinning.

When silk fibre from any of these sources is pre-drafted to a very fine roving, it is very easy to spin using the worsted draw. Here, the fibres are kept lying close together and all in the same direction which means that the natural lustre of silk will remain visible in the finished yarn.

Woollen draw with short silk fibres results in a lacklustre yarn, which has its uses in certain textile designs.

What intrigues most spinners about silk is its warm feel, strength, and lustrous, light-refracting properties. It is a great pleasure when spinning to see how

Spinning silk: worsted draw.

Spinning silk: semi-worsted draw.

Each hankie or cap is made up of fine layers of individual filaments laid one on top of the other. Layers can be identified by looking closely at the outer edge where numerous fibres cling together and form a shiny finish.

1. Carefully pick up a shiny edge and lift one very fine layer off, separating it completely from the remainder. This is not always as easy as it sounds – fibres tend to cling to each other as well as to any rough areas of skin or nails – so hand cream can be helpful here.

2. Once separated, balance the hankie or cap on the thumbs and finger tips of both hands and gradually try to make it bigger by starting at the outer edge and opening out the fingers, forcing your hands further apart as you go. If the hankie will not open up, then the layer was too thick and will need to be separated into two layers. (Remember the fibres are more dense at the outer edge, so concentrate on freeing up these fibres first; the centre will be comparatively easy.)

3. Once the fibres begin to slip over each other and the hankie becomes bigger, you will be left with a circle of fibre.

4. Working with your hands well apart, keep drawing it out until it is possible to separate a fine roving ready for spinning. Break the circle to form one long roving.

5. Spinning is now more a matter of putting in twist and keeping the fibres parallel and of even thickness than a hard learned skill. The secret of success is in the preparation: if the drafting has been efficient it will be possible to smooth out.

light plays on dyed silk fibres as they are fanned and drawn out under tension. Spinning can be with hands held wide apart in an extended worsted technique, or semi-worsted for a very fine, yet strong, yarn.

Spinning silk hankies and caps
Both silk hankies and caps need to be prepared for hand spinning and it is not possible to spin them without carefully drafting out the exceptionally strong fibres beforehand.

The length of thread each layer of silk hankie or cap yields is always much greater than expected. The thread can be incredibly fine and still hold together (i.e. have integrity). But, with silk, this benefit can come at the price of colour.

Silk has an affinity with colour and just loves to take up dye. Hence, deep, vibrant, saturated colours are far more achievable in silk than any other fibre. It is worth remembering, however, that in the spinning, silk is generally spun thin and the colour of any fibre becomes less noticeable as the thread gets thinner. This is due to how the eye reacts to blocks of colour (*see* Chapter 7). This property of colour is more noticeable when spinning silk, for the simple reason that silk can be drawn out more finely than other fibres.

Silk has an affinity with colour.

VEGETABLE FIBRES: CELLULOSE

COTTON

Cotton and flax are currently overlooked as far as hand spinning is concerned. This is surprising as cotton is the most widely used fibre in the world. It comes from the seed pod and its cellulose fibres are short, soft and supple. Fibres are only about 2–3 centimetres long depending on the variety. It is relatively easy to grow and process on industrial scales, so why not use it for hand spinning? The fibre is soft, yet strong, drapes beautifully and takes colour well when it comes to dyeing. Cotton absorbs and wicks moisture and can be combined with other fibres for performance purposes.

For hand spinning, the fibres need to be made into punies by laying the the fibre out carefully onto a blending board and brushing down onto the pins, as illustrated (for wool) in the previous chapter. Starting at the bottom of the board, a few cotton fibres are picked up, trapped between two dowels and rolled into a firm roll, lifting and combing down as described. If the fibres are really short, the puni can be made by lifting it off the blending board as a batt and rolling each puni around a single dowel, rather than two dowels at a time.

Cotton is usually spun to a fairly fine thread and requires a lot of twist. It is good for blending or plying with other fibres. Traditionally, cotton was spun on a charkha wheel which has a very high twist ratio. The direction of twist is always Z when spinning cotton, as S-spun cotton will disintegrate during washing more easily than Z spun.

OTHER PLANT FIBRES

Of the many exotic plant-based fibres, bamboo is probably the most commonly used in hand spinning; it is often seen blended with merino.

On its own, bamboo absorbs moisture and wicks it away from the body far faster than cotton. The plant grows very rapidly, requires little in the way of fertilizer, pesticides and irrigation and so is considered a renewable and sustainable crop. But, as the fibres lie in the stem of the plant, it is not as quickly and easily converted into useable fibre as cotton, which nature provides as a handy flowery seed boll.

Unlike the soft cotton boll, bamboo has a naturally tough, hard stem and turning it into soft fine rovings for hand spinning requires a lot of industrial processing. Industrial processes have a huge environmental impact, from manufacture of the processing machinery in the first instance to the fuel required to run the machinery and local pollution. Harvesting and transport of products to the processing plant, then packaging and transport to the eventual marketplace via wholesaler and retailers all have to be taken into account. This amounts to an extremely high environmental price, which may not be reflected in the retail price due to the variations in world economics.

Most bamboo is converted into bamboo viscose by treating it with chemicals in order to free up the cellulose before further mechanical processing. Although frequently marketed as 'natural bamboo', the environmental impact of these industrial mechanical and chemical processes suggests that in effect it does cost the earth when compared to wool, silk, cotton or flax.

Hackled flax and seeds.

FLAX (LINEN)

Flax, like wool, is another seriously under-used natural, renewable resource that grows on our doorstep. Not many hand spinners spin flax, which is a pity as it compromises neither the welfare of animals nor the environment in which it grows.

Plant fibres that derive from the stems of plants, including flax, hemp, bamboo, ramie and nettle, are known as 'bast' (meaning stem) fibres. Unlike cotton, bast fibres are long, stiff and strong. Left to their own devices, the bast fibres all naturally twist to the left (S twist), but are normally Z spun. Spinning flax is hard work, like the cultivation, harvesting, retting (extracting the fibres by soaking until the green stem has rotted away), which is even more labour intensive. The stems are then scutched to remove debris then pulled through strong sharp hackles to separate the fibres ready for hand spinning.

Flax fibres are naturally hard and tough, so spinning linen (as it becomes known) is harder on the fingers. Spinning is done with wet fingers to help ease the fibres together and reduce friction on the fingers. Hand spun linen can be used with great effect in weaving for both warp and weft and is exceptionally strong.

Linen was traditionally spun very finely for weaving (the finer the better) and one can only feel great respect for those whose livelihood depended on this arduous way of life in the past. Many old spinning wheels have small bobbins and a tiny (<5 mm) orifice. This is a tell-tale sign of a flax wheel, particularly if there is a distaff attached. (But do not be fooled by such a spinning wheel, as these things are not necessarily any proof of antiquity!) It is perfectly possible to spin flax on any spinning wheel regardless of orifice size. Where an orifice is too large and causes vibration then a grommet fitted tightly inside the orifice will reduce its diameter and prevent the fibre moving rapidly from side to side, which causes vibration when the wheel is turning quickly.

Making and dressing a distaff

Before spinning, the flax fibre needs to be 'dressed' onto a supporting framework known as a distaff. This can be a home-made, cone-shaped construction made of strong paper, stuffed with newspaper and stuck together with sticky tape.

A distaff of about 14–16 inches tall fits the natural length of the flax. It resembles a witch's hat and can be mounted on a broom handle – more fairytale-like than ever! When ready for use, the broom handle is tied to a chair leg (in two places, or it will wobble).

Distaffs can also be made from wire frameworks or wooden structures that fit onto the spinning wheel.

A distaff allows individual fibres to be drawn off for spinning. Getting fibres onto the distaff is called 'dressing'.

The aim of dressing a distaff is to enable fibres to be pulled off for spinning at a rate of one or two at a time without getting into a tangle.

Fibres are attached the opposite way to which the plant grows; the root ball is at the top and the tips of the fibres hang downwards. The rootball and fibre tips look very similar but can be distinguished by feel as the rootball is much more coarse to the touch. To assemble the fibres:

1. Take a ribbon, long enough to go round the waist, and tie in a bow.
2. Tie the fibre bunch by the root ball in the middle of the ribbon and then tie the ribbon around your waist like an apron so that the fibres are securely fixed in front of you.
3. Sit down, and place an apron or large towel over your knees and let the fibres hang down towards your left side (if you are right handed).
4. Hold the fibre bunch with your left hand and gently ease off a few fibres.
5. Without breaking the fibres away from their root ball, spread them evenly all over your lap, separating them out as you go. Make sure they are clearly separated from other fibres in the bunch, but still attached by their stems at the root ball.
6. Repeat the process with a few more fibres, laying them out across your lap on top of the previous layer.
7. Gradually build up an arc of fibres with the tips hanging over your knees and the stems still attached at the root ball tied round your waist.
8. Untie the root ball from around your waist and gently lift the whole arc-shaped network of flax, along with the towel or apron that supports it underneath, on to a table.

9. Now, lay the distaff over the arc of prepared fibre with the narrow top part at the root ball and roll the fibres onto the distaff folding the tips upward and tucking them in to make a neat edge at the bottom as you roll it round.
10. Before moving it off the table, tie the fibres at the top of the distaff as tightly as you can in the middle of the long length of ribbon (or lace), leaving two ends as before.
11. Working from the top down, wrap the ribbon ends and criss-cross them over each other so that the fibres are held in place and cannot slip or fall off.
12. Tie the ribbon in a neat bow at the bottom.
13. The distaff can now be mounted on its stand so that it is about shoulder height when the spinner is sitting down. If using a home-made distaff remember to tie it securely to the chair leg in at least two places, otherwise it will wobble when you start to draw down the fibre.

The colour of the distaff lace or ribbon is said to be significant as tradition has it that this denoted the status of the spinner: single, betrothed or married.

The word 'distaff' is still associated with the female side of the family and the term 'spinster' referred to a spinner of single status who was not considered ready to be married until she could spin a quality yarn. The following poem, discovered in *Good Housekeeping*, Volume 2 (1885), suggests the colour of distaff ribbon was a matter for consideration, whether its significance was real or imagined.

Careful separation of each fibre when dressing the distaff facilitates spinning a consistently fine, smooth thread.

'The Song of the Distaff',
by G.P. Grantham

Thy distaff take, of the ribbon white;
Spin, spin for thine own true knight
The plaited shirt he shall one day wear,
When thou shalt become his bride so fair.

Thy distaff take, of the ribbon blue;
Spin, spin, with devotion true
And humble prayer, his priestly vest,
Whose hands shall join you in wedlock blest.

Thy distaff take, of the ribbon green;
Spin, spin, with a fervour keen,
The cloth, where scores of us then will throng,
To drink, and to raise the nuptial song.

Thy distaff take, of the ribbon gray;
Spin, spin the broad curtains gay
For bridal chamber and nuptial bower,
Dear Love's refection, and Virtue's dower.

Thy distaff take, of the ribbon of gold;
Spin, spin, with a pride untold,
Weaving small robes with maternal joy,
And swathing-bands for thy first bright boy.

Thy distaff take, of the ribbon red;
Spin, spin of the daintiest thread
A kerchief fair, thy tears to keep,
And dry thine eyes when thou fain wouldst weep.

Thy distaff take, of the ribbon black;
Spin, spin, ere thy powers slack,
The winding-sheet thou must one day win,
That one of us here will enwrap thee in.

Flax is best kept moist when spinning.
Dampening the fibres releases a natural gum
which helps keep ends together.

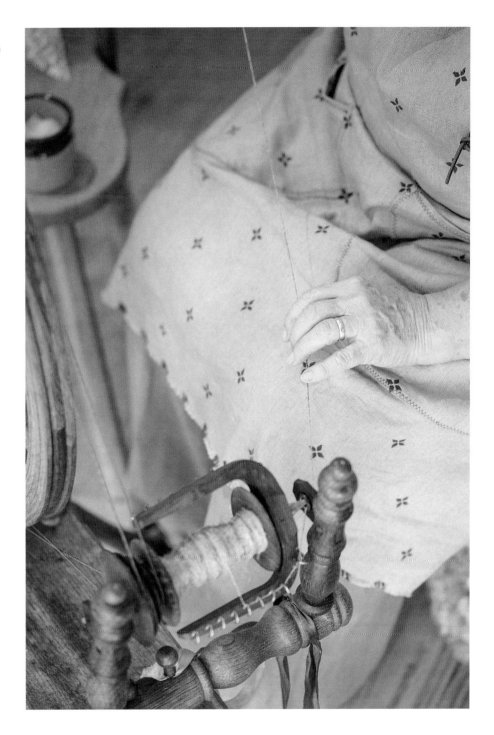

Spinning flax

Spinning flax is a good 'spectator sport' as the wheel and dressed distaff trigger a fairytale image. The flow of flax from the distaff through the spinner's hands and onto the bobbin is continuous and the process is easy to understand for those watching.

Spinning is very calm and peaceful and the wheel seldom needs to stop turning at the hands of a competent long draw spinner. Whereas a full bobbin of wool will weigh 100g, a bobbin of flax will contain two or three times that weight, if the wheel's drive mechanism is strong enough to keep the bobbin turning. As a result, bobbins do not need to be changed so often. Spun flax is quite stable in its single state, unlike other fibres which need plying to make them manageable.

For spinning, the distaff needs to be mounted to the right-hand side of the spinner at a convenient height to draw off a few fibres at a time.

Flax is spun with wet fingers to help ease the loose fibres ends together and reduce friction on the balls of the finger tips. A small pot of water (a sponge inside the pot avoids splashes and spills) can be placed on the stock of the wheel if the stock stands horizontally, or suspended from the wheel with string tied round the rim. Spinning is traditionally Z, clockwise direction.

The prepared flax stems are presented as individual fibres for the twist to be added. Twist in flax is not as mobile as in fleece of animal fibre.

Spinning flax requires a combination of spinning techniques: both long worsted and forward draw, depending on how the fibre comes off the distaff. The fibres are about 18 inches long so hands needs to be wide apart to enable fibres to be drawn out where necessary. Flax fibre – or linen as it is now known – is extremely strong and cannot be broken if it gets in a tangle, so it is best to work at avoiding

this happening in the first place. When a snag happens, no amount of strength will resolve it; the fibres must be separated out and drawn away.

Thread will be hairy unless care is taken to draw out fibres and ensure that fibre tips and ends are wound into the thread; spinning with wet fingers helps bring this about. The flax responds well to moisture and is much easier to spin and smooth out when very slightly damp. Loose fibre ends are not just unsightly but cause problems in weaving as they build up and get stuck in the reeds and heddles, reducing the thickness of the fibre. The aim is to create a consistently smooth thread. It has no stretch so is not suitable for knitting or crochet.

The preparation of combing out hackled flax, and separating fibres when dressing the distaff, makes the spinning feel like a comparatively simple operation. The skill in spinning flax depends on a smooth, continuous flow of fibre from

Linen in plain weave with leno border inset (by F. Frances).

Handmade table linen makes a unique wedding gift.

the distaff, hence the skill in dressing it and separating out the fibres. If the distaff has been carefully prepared, this will be easy and the supporting ribbon or lace can be tightened as necessary to hold the remaining fibres in place. Flax fibre is long, strong, and quite unforgiving to spin. The aim in spinning is to achieve a continuous flow of fibre from the distaff that can be drawn out into a consistent, finely spun thread.

The next stage is to weave the linen thread and, finally, the fabric is finished by boiling it in water. Initially, it is a pale grey or golden colour and, the more it is boiled, the more white it becomes.

In Victorian times, all linen towels, sheets and table cloths and napkins were boiled as part of the standard domestic laundry process, the purpose being to make the linen white, as well as remove stains and bacteria. Such boilers, up to a metre in diameter, were made of copper and can be seen in museums or polished and in use as decorative containers for flowers or logs in hotels and country houses.

Weaving linen requires a great deal more skill than weaving wool. The warp threads need to be treated (sized) to help them slip through the heddles and reeds without shredding. The finer the sett, the more likely the chance of shredding. There is no 'forgiveness' in weaving linen because there is no stretch in the thread, and the least little inconsistency will show. But then so will the most intricate of weave patterns, so this can be seen as an advantage.

Weaving can be done on a rigid heddle or traditional loom with 2–16 shafts. However, the time it takes to spin the fibre and then warp up and size a loom and weave it, usually means that a table runner or set of napkins is a big enough project to satisfy even the most ambitious spinner.

And the nature of flax is such that it will not wear out – probably not ever in your lifetime. Nor will it shrink or be eaten by moths. The more linen is used and laundered, the softer and whiter it becomes. So, unlike other things in life, age enhances rather than decays

it. Furthermore, handmade table linen can be in use all the time, so the joy of using your handiwork can become part of everyday life.

With the growing interest in organic food, organic tableware such as handspun and hand-woven linen makes a rare and superbly apposite gift – a priceless compliment which cannot be purchased from the supermarket shelf.

The traditional association of flax with the female side of the family and events of family life makes handmade linen a perfect wedding gift.

IN A NUTSHELL

What we spin, the products we make, and the use we then make of them during a lifetime, transcends commonplace values. Spinners were mindful long before 'mindfulness' became a buzz word, and before diminishing world resources and animal welfare became an international cause for concern.

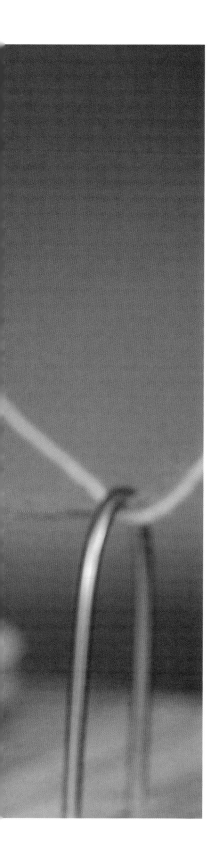

6 Plying and Finishing Yarn

There is no moment more memorable to a hand spinner than holding one's first skein of hand-spun yarn. Spinning the bobbins may have been a major work of determination and grit, but compared to spinning, plying is easy. Here, we look at the tools, tips and tricks necessary to transform a bobbin of singles thread into a beautifully finished skein. But first you need to know which way the twist lies…

DIRECTION OF TWIST

Knowing which way to twist when plying is paramount, as it must be in the opposite direction to which it was spun. Ply the same way as spinning, and your lovingly spun yarn will spring into a useless frenzied tangle the moment it is set free – by which time it will be too late to put matters right.

Being able to see the direction of twist is what really counts because this dictates which way to turn the wheel or spindle when plying. The direction must always be opposite to the way it was spun, or previously plied.

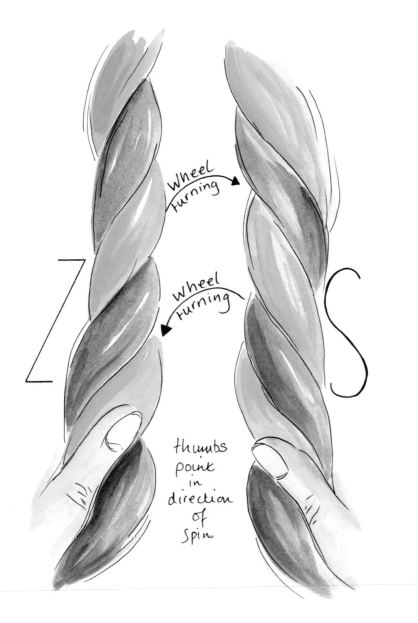

Wheel turning

Wheel turning

thumbs point in direction of spin

POINTING THUMBS

For those who find the 'S or Z' method of determining twist confusing, there are other methods. As the illustration demonstrates, it is far easier to let your thumbs show the way the wheel was turning when the twist went in.

Simply place the thread in front of you on a table and just let your hands rest palm downwards either side of it. Look at your thumbs and align them with the twist in the thread. One or other thumb will align with the thread and show the direction of twist. On the left hand the thumb points to the right (like the centre stem in the letter Z). Turning the spinning wheel in the direction your thumb is pointing will result in Z twist, i.e. traditional spinning direction. Conversely, your right thumb will be pointing to the left, the traditional direction for plying. Run a top whorl spindle down the left leg for spinning and down the right leg for plying.

The way the thumb points shows which way the wheel turned when making the thread or yarn. If it is a singles thread and you want to ply it, then turn the wheel in the opposite direction. If you want to spin more singles, just the same way, then turn the wheel the way your thumb points. It is not necessary to use 'S' or 'Z' terminology, but once you have mastered the thumb test, the terminology seems less complex.

On a top whorl spindle, to ply or spin in S direction, set it spinning by running it down the right leg. Just look at the direction of your thumbs and that will tell you which way the wheel was turning when the thread was spun. And ply the opposite.

S OR Z?

In industry, twist direction is referred to as S or Z. Although it is not essential to know your S from your Z, it is necessary to know which way the twist is lying, i.e. which way the wheel was turning when the yarn was made. Otherwise you will not know in which direction to turn your wheel to carry out the next stage of yarn construction. Surprisingly, recognizing the direction of twist is a rare skill amongst hand spinners!

To view the direction of twist, look at the illustration, or hold a thread vertically, in suspension; it will be the same viewed upside down – despite what many think!

The definition derives from the direction of the centre stem of the two letters. In the letter S the centre stem lies from top left to bottom right; in the letter Z, it lies from bottom left to top right.

READING AS A BOOK

Pick up a book, and your eye naturally goes to the top left-hand side of the page to start reading (unless reading Arabic text which is read from right to left). This method is so instinctive that it is an easy way of reading twist.

Hold the thread, vertically, and look closely at the left-hand side; reading like a book, ask yourself, 'is this twist dangling down like a snake from the left-hand side of the yarn?' If so, it is S. Or, does the twist look like a ladder (Z), leaning up against the right-hand side of the page?

Happily, there are only two things to remember: dangling downwards or leaning to the right. If its dangling, then it is S for snake. If not, it must be Z, leaning like a ladder towards the right-hand side.

ANDEAN PLYING

The easiest way to ply small amounts of thread is with the Andean method. Here the yarn will end up back on the same bobbin or spindle without needing any other equipment. Andean yields 2-ply; there is no need to wind off into two equal balls, or spin two separate bobbins before you can ply.

Just as the quick way to start spinning is with a drop spindle, so it is with Andean plying. Learn this little trick, and it will save a lot of hassle when you want to test a small sample. Likewise when there is a small amount of singles left on the bobbin it can be made into 2 ply; for 3 ply use the Navajo method below.

The method is to transfer the thread from the bobbin or spindle onto the left hand in such a way that it does not tangle

Bobbins mounted vertically on a Lazy Kate are less likely to tip.

2-ply yarn lying at an angle of about 45 degrees looks 'comfortable with itself'.

when it comes off again. When it is transferred, the two ends of the single thread are put together, re-attached to the wheel or spindle and twisted together (plied) in the opposite direction to which they were spun. The way in which the thread is wrapped is critical; any mistakes here will make a tangled mass rather than a stable yarn. It is equally important to be able to find the beginning of the thread when it is all transferred to the hand so, at the outset, this needs to be carefully secured.

Although Andean plying is a simple technique, it is possible to get into a muddle when you first try it. It is worth practising with a ball of left-over commercial yarn; this will save putting your precious hand-spun singles at risk. It is wise to ply small quantities at a time, for the same reason. Lengths can be easily joined together by looping them through the end of the previous batch which is always a loop; i.e. the mid-point of the original singles. The yarn can then be made into a skein for final washing and finishing.

ANDEAN PLY

STEP 1   Take hold of the thread, either from the bobbin and through the orifice, or directly from the spindle. Secure the end of the thread around the little finger of the *left* hand; you will need to find the end later so it is important that the end is not lost.

STEP 2   With your right hand, take the thread across your palm, over your (left) thumb and wrap it all the way round the back of your hand. It is important to maintain the same direction; thread will form a cross below the middle finger.

STEP 3   Maintaining the same direction, take the thread over your palm and up between your first and middle finger; wrap it all the way around the middle finger of the left hand; make sure it goes all the way round the finger and continues in the same clockwise direction all the time.

STEP 4   Now, take the thread over your palm towards your thumb and wrap it all the way round the back of your hand as before. Continue wrapping, making sure it is not too tight; you will need to be able to pull it off your finger later on.

STEP 5 Keep wrapping in the same, clockwise, direction – all the way round the finger, all the way round the hand, round the finger, round the hand – until you get to the end of the thread. There will be no crossover of thread at the back of the hand.

STEP 6 Now, pull all the loops that are round your middle finger off, and leave them in the palm of your hand.

STEP 7 Leave the remainder on your wrist. Locate both ends, and secure both ends to the leader thread on your wheel, or hook of the spindle.

STEP 8 Turning the wheel or spindle anticlockwise for S twist, i.e. the *opposite* direction in which it was spun, ply the two threads together, letting the threads pull from your left hand as required. (Rolling your spindle down the right leg (S twist) is the only option, because the left hand contains the yarn!)

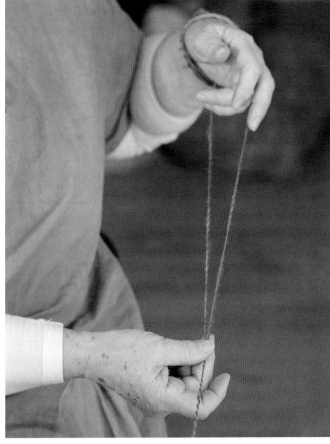

LAZY KATE: 2 OR MORE PLY

A simpler method of plying from two or three bobbins involves mounting the bobbins on a device known as a Lazy Kate, which allows thread to be drawn off without tangling, as the bobbins rotate.

Some Lazy Kates incorporate a Scotch tension to prevent bobbins from spinning backwards due to a sudden change of tension from the spinner's hands or the wheel.

A Lazy Kate will usually accommodate two or three bobbins; those which hold bobbins in an upright position, on a large flat base, are less likely to tip over the one-above-the-other design.

To make a Lazy Kate, simply take a strong box such as a shoe box and pierce holes opposite each other – more than a bobbin width apart – down the long side. Bobbins can then be suspended on old knitting needles, and a fine tensioner thread tied around the box lengthwise so that it fits in the bobbin grooves.

For 2 or 3 ply the threads from each bobbin are tied to the leader and then, turning the wheel anticlockwise (i.e. the opposite direction to the spinning direction), twisted together evenly.

Ideally, there will be similar amounts of thread on the bobbins. If there is doubt, weighing them will give an indication. However, when in 2 ply mode, any thread remaining on one bobbin can be Andean plied, to use up any leftover yarn on a bobbin.

When two threads are plied together, the yarn is quite a different texture from three. Three threads lie in closer proximity to each other than two, which can only ever be side by side. This trinity of yarn creates a more solid, cord-like structure, and because it involves three threads is usually quite a bit thicker.

NAVAJO PLY

Another way to make 3-ply yarn is to use the Navajo technique which uses just one bobbin at a time.

This is particularly useful when spinning yarn where the colour keeps changing (see Rainbow Dyeing) as it maintains the same colour sequence; without it, the colour changes would become muddled and, quite possibly, 'mudded' (see Chapter 7). When spinning punis, where blending is often the dominant feature, a Navajo ply will maintain the subtle gradations in colour hue, which would be virtually impossible if using two different bobbins.

Navajo ply is simply a series of chain loops, as in crochet. Long loops with the right hand, and controlling twist with the left, will help avoid getting into a tangle with Navajo ply.

HOW MUCH TWIST?

The amount of twist per inch cannot possibly be specified for every type of yarn or fibre; even less can it be consistently produced in hand spinning. Be realistic, not mechanistic, remembering that hand-spun yarn needs to be fit for the purpose, rather than matching criteria designed for commercial manufacturing. To apply a rule of so many twists per inch (tpi) throughout a whole skein of hand-spun yarn is just as unrealistic as saying you must drive your car at exactly 30mph throughout a journey. It cannot be done. At best, tpi, like mph, can only ever be an average.

Can anyone count twist, correlated to a measured distance, treadle a wheel (in the correct direction) and handle two or three singles threads, all at the same time? And, factor in how much twist is lost when the flyer is winding on and the bobbin not turning? No! Precision of this degree is best left to commercial manufacturing.

There can be too little or too much twist in a yarn, as we will see, but there is huge divergence between these two poles. The following information is for guidance only and the 'eyeball test' and common sense are highly recommended.

Far too many spinners lose confidence or undervalue their yarn because it does not meet the unrealistic criteria used in commercial production. So, be brave, and, like Jonathan Livingston Seagull*, don't follow the flock: follow your instinct, learn as much as you can, be adventurous and

---

* Richard Bach, *Jonathan Livingston Seagull*. A fable about a seagull who went against convention and the rules of his flock, and learned to fly better than any other seagull.

3-ply yarn has a stronger, more cord-like texture, than 2-ply.

Navajo creates a 3-ply yarn in a series of chains as in crochet. It is ideal for yarn spun in progressive colours.

NAVAJO PLY

STEP 1   Place the full bobbin on a Lazy Kate, positioned to the right of your wheel, and put an empty bobbin with a leader thread with a loop in it, on the flyer.

STEP 2   Tie a long loop in the singles – big enough to get your hand through. Thread this through the loop of your leader thread that is on the bobbin.

STEP 3   Holding the thread with your left hand, make another large loop through your first loop by putting your right hand right through the first loop, grabbing the thread, and pulling it through the loop to create the next one.

STEP 4   Now, turn the wheel slowly, remembering to go anti-clockwise. Hold the thread at the loop so that three strands are between your left hand and the wheel and watch as the twist goes in.

STEP 5   Pinch the thread and hold back the twist with your left hand as you pull through each loop; otherwise the thread will twist right up to the end and close the next loop.

STEP 6   When the loop is made, allow the twist into the yarn by sliding the left hand along the thread as far as the next position i.e. the next loop.

try things out. This is how knowledge is extended. The correct, or 'proper' way to spin, is the way that suits the spinner.

Philosophy aside, there are some unquestionable facts of spinning life. Firstly, there is an inverse relationship between fibre and twist – and this is true in plying as well as spinning. The more fibre you have, the less twist you need, and vice versa.

A 2-ply yarn will accommodate a lot more twist per inch than a 3-ply, so it is necessary to turn the wheel far more slowly when making 3-ply. In the amount of ply needed for a balanced yarn, the thickness of the yarn plays a far greater part than most spinners anticipate.

A guideline for the amount of twist a yarn should have is to examine the angle at which the ply is lying in a short length of ply. An angle of 45 degrees (half a right angle) is generally considered comfortable. As the angle becomes more acute, the likelihood of the yarn being over-plied increases. Conversely, if the ply is lying at an angle far greater than 45 degrees, it is likely to be under-plied and, in places, loose fibres will visibly be untwisting themselves.

THE EYEBALL TEST

Your personal critical assessment is likely to be good enough in the early stages of learning to spin. Just look at the yarn and ask yourself some questions: does the yarn look 'comfortable'? If there were more, or less, twist, would it be more likely to wear well, feel good, or look good? Which is more likely to fluff and pill in wear? Which will feel hard or soft?

Is it worth testing a tiny sample of what you have done so far – just as an exercise in learning? You decide.

A guideline of how many treadles/length is given below. But, for the moment, rough judgement and common sense will suffice. Even the most inexperienced knitters and spinners can tell, by the look and feel of the yarn, if it is comfortable with itself. Far better to use your intuition and allow instinct to play its natural part in your hand spinning, than to try to follow a prescription. The experience is all part of becoming a hand spinner.

DOUBLING

As a first pass in plying, or 'doubling' as it was known, there is a useful little trick which children find fascinating, especially if the yarn is in two different colours. It is also handy if you want to see what your yarn will look like when plied.

Simply spin an arm's length of thick yarn, changing the colour of the fibre half way, and fold the length in half. You need three hands for this trick, so try holding the length between your two hands and hooking it over the nearest maiden (the upright part which supports the flyer) at the mid-point.

Now bring the two ends together in one hand and take hold of the mid-point with the other hand. Let go of the middle, and the yarn plies itself! It is transformed into a strong, stable yarn. This is the bit the children love to see; they happily tie them on as wristbands – especially if they have twirled the thread themselves on a drop spindle.

CONSISTENCY

A yarn that is inconsistent is not necessarily fit for its purpose, making it a poor quality yarn. Inconsistency can make life difficult; just because a yarn is hand spun doesn't mean one is forced to knit every inch of it!

Some twist in the singles is lost in plying, so a degree of over-twist in the singles is helpful. If a plied yarn is under-plied in one place and over-plied in another, it will be quite impractical to use – at least, in normal circumstances.

To achieve consistency in plying requires a degree of control which, boring as it may seem, means having to count the number of treadles that go into a set length of thread. When the optimum number of treadles is known, it is easy to develop a rhythm and, consistently, replicate it.

First, make a ply that looks and feels comfortable with itself, i.e. it passes your eyeball test or other predetermined measure, such as making a smooth arc and not doubling back on itself when allowed to hang freely in a loop between two hands. It can be useful to tie a sample between the spokes of the spinning wheel to use for reference; but make sure the twist remains in the sample as new twist never wants to stay put. Now, replicate the ply over a set length, say 3 feet, counting the number of times you press down the treadle as you do so.

On an Ashford Traditional at standard spin setting, between 4 and 6 treadles for every yard of 2-ply, is often about right for double knit weight yarn.

The objective is to achieve a plied yarn with a desired amount of twist that is con-

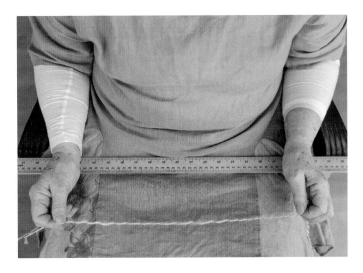

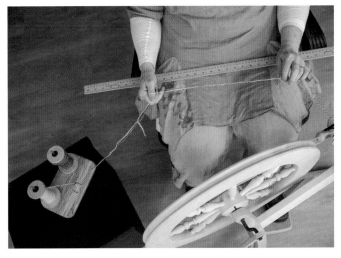

Twist is measured over distance – twists per inch of yarn (tpi). To achieve a consistent ply, count the number of treadles (twist) per set length of yarn.

A chair with arms facilitates keeping an even tension over a repeatable set distance without the need for a ruler; all that is necessary then, is to count the number of treadles and allow for winding on. Avoid acute angles between bobbins and orifice.

sistent throughout the skein. It is important to realize that two things needs to be considered here: twist and distance.

Knowing the ratio of twist per treadle is useful, but what counts is the number of treadles over a given length of yarn. Knowing the ratio of turns per treadle is of little significance if you cannot control the number of treadles that go into a set length of yarn.

To get the amount of twist you want, think in terms of treadles per set length, rather than trying to count twists per inch. Measuring out the 50cm or so of singles for consistent plying is made easier if you sit in an upright chair that has arms.

Resting your arms on the chair will keep the distance constant without having to think about it all the time. On a standard chair, with your arms resting, the distance between your two hands will

probably be about 50cm. So, count the number of treadles it takes to give the amount of twist you require. It could be as few as three for a thick yarn or lots more for a very fine yarn.

There are too many variables to predict an exact figure but, if it takes, say, five treadles to get the yarn to look and behave as you wish, then you know how many to use each time for each length.

Allow one turn of the treadle to feed the length in, onto the bobbin. Do this as quickly as possible to avoid putting in more twist than you need. Now measure out the next length, treadle the correct number of times, let the twist in, and store the yarn.

This method will give a consistent ply.

It is essential to hold the single threads under the same tension when plying a standard 2- or 3-ply yarn. In bouclé, coils

and designer yarns in different tensions are used for effect (*see* Chapter 9) but, for standard plying, try to maintain equal tension on each thread all the time.

It is helpful to place the Lazy Kate to the right of the spinning wheel and slightly behind you. Avoid acute angles between the bobbins and the orifice and try to keep the thread travelling in as straight a line as possible, as this will help avoid thread getting caught or snagging on the rim of the bobbins. Hold the yarn so that each singles has its own separate pathway between the fingers of the right hand. In this way the tension can be controlled, avoiding any 'squirmals' where the yarn plies back on itself when slackened.

Aim for even tension on all threads at all times, to achieve a yarn that looks comfortable with itself, with no loose, free fibres and no tight coils.

SKEINING AND FINISHING

Although the newly plied yarn is fairly stable on the bobbin, it will need a final wash before it looks its best.

Even if the fibre was clean to start with, washing is still necessary as this has the effect of evening out inconsistencies in twist and loosens the fibres to make an even, lofty yarn. Washing is best done in the skein and, as it dries, the twist sets into place.

Should the yarn be under-twisted it can be slightly felted and re-skeined to make it more reliable. Or, more twist can be put in by repeating the previous process. But first, make a skein.

Before removing from the Niddy-Noddy, yarn must be secured in several different places with loosely tied figure-of-eight loops.

MAKING A SKEIN

A skein can be made by wrapping the yarn around the back of an armchair. First make sure the shape of the chair back will accommodate removing the skein, particularly as winding may be tighter than intended!

When all the yarn is gently wrapped, tie the two ends together, otherwise it can be difficult to find the ends again. DO NOT attempt to remove the skein from the chair until it is secured in at least three of four places with loose figure-of-eight ties. These ties are traditionally done with left-over singles from the plying, which is aesthetically pleasing in the final presentation.

Skeins can be made, more easily, with specialized equipment such as a Niddy-Noddy. On average, one pass round a Niddy-Noddy will be 1.5–2 yards. In this way, it is possible to calculate the length of yarn in the skein by measuring the distance around it (after it is washed and set – see below) and multiplying it by the number of loops in the skein. Skeins of 100 or 150 yards, or metres, make estimating the amount of yarn needed for a project more straightforward.

SETTING THE TWIST

The newly plied skein will be even more lovely when it is washed and the twist set as it dries.

Even though the wool may have already been washed before spinning, the second wash is necessary too.

At this stage, the woollen fibres seem to loosen up, fluff or settle together, depending on the way it was spun.

Wash the skein as you would any woollen garment that you don't want to shrink, in warm water without much agitation. Remmeber that heat and friction will cause a yarn to felt, as will a sudden change of temperature or shock. So, keep the washing and rinsing water temperature more or less the same. Do not agitate strongly and handle the yarn gently.

Wring it out by hand and hang it up to dry with a little bit of tension such as from a can of beans or weight of some sort suspended from the skein. As it dries, the twist will set in place under this slight tension.

Strong direct sunlight can also cause felting so this is best avoided. Should the yarn felt slightly, this is not a serious problem, and is unlikely to have a major impact on anything except the yardage. There are times, such as when a yarn may lack strength, when it is desirable to felt slightly to improve its strength – or 'integrity' as it is known in spinning.

LABEL AND ADMIRE!

When the skein is dry, hold both ends and twist tightly with one hand. Fold in half and the skein will double back on itself. Tuck one end into the other.

Label, to record the fibre source, spin method, and date. And then sit back and appreciate the work of your hands!

REALISTIC CRITICAL ASSESSMENT

The process of hand spinning has always been so commonplace that it did not need to be written down. It was the everyday business of the lower classes and therefore was of little interest to educated writers such as Cicero, whose detailed records of rhetoric, philoso-

Information about yarn can be recorded on the back of personalized tags.

Traditional skein presentation (by V. Kemp).

phy and administration are still with us today. In the nineteenth century, with the Industrial Revolution, the practice moved from home to factory, but, more recently, spinning has returned to the home – bringing with it unrealistic commercial standards, such as so many twists per inch and artificial consistency. Very few spinners have the luxury of unlimited time to pursue their interest to the level of academic excellence – worthy as this is. Most fit spinning around working hours, caring for children or the elderly, and the other demands of life.

Hand-spun yarn is totally different from commercial yarn, however. Hand spinners are discerning, creative, responsive, inspired people who love wool; no commercial process can match that! Spinning practice is continually evolving and it is mostly new spinners with open minds who make this happen.

IN A NUTSHELL

There is nothing wrong in taking pleasure in your handiwork; it need not be out of vanity, but for critical appreciation of your work, your standards, your achievement and your pleasure. Touch it, feel it, smell it, squeeze it. All these things tell a spinner something about the yarn, as well as being a pleasure. Even after years and miles and miles of spinning, the joy of holding your own newly hand-spun yarn never ceases. To create yarn from fleece implies no carbon footprint, no harsh processing or chemical contaminants. Nothing had to die or was poisoned to create pure hand-spun yarn. Pure joy!

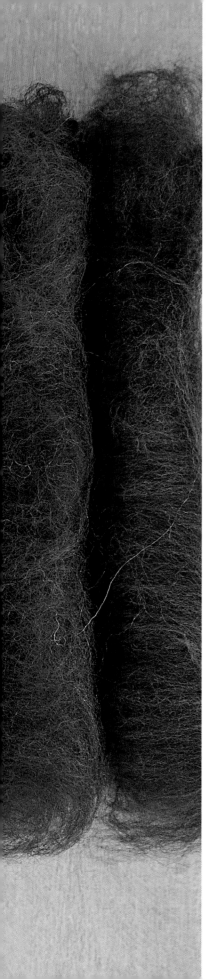

7 Colour in Spinning

All spinners make choices about colour – even those who think they are not very good with colour. For these spinners, this chapter will show you how to learn some colour skills, to take control and discover just how much fun colour can be. You do not have to be 'gifted' in some special way. The accepted wisdom from colour theorists makes it easy, and there are some hand-painted colour charts to re-create in yarn or provide inspiration.

Having mastered spinning and fibre preparation, learning to work with colour in spinning is the next natural step. There is no mystique about working with colour once you understand how colours react to one another and to light (or lack of it).

Eyes pick up primary colours – known as 'hues' – and our brains make sense of the mixes, in much the same way that ears pick up sounds and brains make sense of those sounds.

Admittedly, there are a few very talented colourists, as there are talented musicians and other artists. But the majority of people enjoy music without being musicians, and it is the same with colour – most of us can engage with it.

First, a word about the words used in the language of colour. It is easy to be intimidated by unfamiliar words and quite unfair to use them without explanation.

- Rain - COLOURS of EARTH - forests -

Moors - Heather - Azure - Twilight - Lavender - Mist -

Lake - Teal - Pine - Fir - Ochre - Sand - Bay

Sage - Berry - Rose - chestnut

- For *hue*, read, 'colour family', such as the red family.
- For *saturation*, think, 'as much colour as it can take' – an 'intense' yellow, or 'vibrant' purple.
- *Neutral* colours are black, brown, white, grey.
- A *monochromatic* colour has had some white, grey or black added to make it lighter, duller or darker than the original.
- The three *primary* colours – red, yellow and blue – are the most vibrant in their pure state. As primary colours are mixed, whether in fibre, paint, ink or crayon, the less saturated (vibrant, intense, or 'in-your-face') they become.

It is useful to see how all colours originate from the three primary colours. Mix up one of the secondary colours with a primary and you will find what are known as the tertiary colours. Tertiary colours are blue-green, blue-violet, red-violet, red-orange, yellow-green, yellow-orange, which are also frequently referred to as hues. Should you let all the primary and secondary colours muddle up together the end result would look like mud.

Primary colours are fine for nursery school children but nothing would induce most spinners to wear or work with such colours. With maturity, our brains become more discerning and, the more time we spend with colour, the more sensitive we become to it. Most adults are attracted to colours that are more sophisticated than primary colours. Spinners often want something lighter, duller, softer or more subtle, as opposed to a colour that is 'in-your-face' or 'making a statement'.

The first engagement with colour, for a spinner, usually comes with a coloured fibre which just doesn't feel right. It is not a question of putting two colours together but, knowing how to adjust the colour, so that it is comfortable to work with, wear or give as a gift.

The uncertainty is where confidence with colour can rapidly drain away, particularly when you do are unfamiliar with the language colour theorists use.

TINTS, TONES AND SHADES

Sooner or later, all spinners end up with fibre or yarn which is the 'wrong' colour. Knowing how to modify a colour within predictable or safe parameters does wonders for the confidence.

Think of 'tints, tones and shades' as a tool in a toolbox of tricks that works for one colour (like a spanner only works with a nut – it will not undo a screw). Because of this, it is the easiest colour skill to grasp and, probably, the most useful. It enables the intensity of a colour to be changed with predictable results.

The technique is demonstrated here with fine quality merino roving using fine 119ppi hand carders. The basic principle also works when plying yarns: to modify the colour simply ply with white, grey or black as required. As white is not an option with dye, only the concepts of tones and shades have implications for dyeing.

TINTS

If the colour is too intense or too dark, this can be adjusted by putting more 'light' in. To do this, add a small quantity of similar fine white roving, say 20 percent of the original weight of colour and mix by carding with hand carders, a drum carder, or by blending on a blending board. If your original colour was a warm acid yellow, it will now be a much lighter, soft yellow. In the same way a red will become pink, and blue will become a pastel blue suitable for a baby.

TONES

Sometimes, the colour you want is fine as far as light or dark is concerned, but is simply too intense, vibrant or 'saturated', as colourists would say. In this case, use a similar quality grey fibre to take out some of the colour but keep the original degree of light/darkness (greyscale).

SHADES

Without light, there is no colour at all. So, if a colour is too 'in-your-face' bright and intense, put some black in. Choose the same quality fibre in black and add a very small quantity, less than 10 percent of the original weight of colour, and mix by carding with hand carders or a drum carder or blending on a blending board. If your original colour was acid yellow, it will turn into a lovely olive green. Hot red will become a sophisticated plum colour, and royal blue a classy navy.

Grey Tints

Phantom - Hush - Spindrift - Spray - Breath -

Haze - Mist - Mizzle - Drizzle - Fog -

- Cool - Pool - Night - Shade -

Rolags in saturated blue, red, and yellow merino lie crosswise over a 30% blend of white (tint), grey (tone) or black (shade).

LIGHT AND DARK SHADES OF GREY

The concept of greyscale is a subtle tool in managing colour. Greyscale describes the light or darkness of a colour as if it were a shade of grey and not a colour at all. Think of it as helping to assess just how light or dark a colour is, not the colour family it belongs to.

To express a colour in terms of a shade of grey sounds rather strange but, if you look at a black-and-white TV or photograph, you can easily distinguish the different colours you know are there because they appear as many different shades of grey in the photo.

An exact measure of greyscale is particularly useful when using more than one colour or bringing several colours together within the same project.

Colourists and fibre artists meas-ure greyscale from within a range of 0 (where 0 is white) up to 10, or sometimes 12, which is completely black.

Greyscale measures are available commercially as *shade cards* with holes in that can be matched up with the shade of grey in question; hold the card over the colour to identify the nearest match or what it would look like in a black-and-white photograph.

Now that cameras are to hand on the mobile phone, it is a useful habit to take a black-and-white photo of fibres when selecting them for a yarn or project. Greyscale can be quickly assessed in this way and the effects adjusted at the design stage. Dark colours that are also at the dark end of the grey scale will appear somewhat sombre, which can be dramatic – or boring. The black-and-white photo will soon show this up.

Subtle colours in the middle range of greyscale tend to feel more peaceful, while those at the light end create interest and energy. Again, it is a question of balance; the greyscale measure is a uniquely influential tool for working with colour.

MIXING COLOURS AS FIBRE OR YARN

THE ARTIST'S COLOUR WHEEL

Putting colours together in a yarn or project where it will remain for ever, can be a daunting prospect. Musicians don't have to live with their discordant efforts: the music is played and gone in a moment of time! Alas, for spinners the evidence remains and they have to live with their mistakes until they can bear them no longer! Thankfully, the artist's colour wheel helps avoid glaring errors;

Greyscale is easy to see in this black-and-white photograph of rolags made of tints, tones and shades of primary colours.

Colour photograph of rolags made of tints, tones and shades of primary colours.

Devices such as this 'Pocket Colour Wheel' take some of the uncertainty out of working with colour.

hence it is the most indispensable item in the toolbox.

The inexpensive Pocket Colour Wheel features three primary, three secondary, and six tertiary colours (twelve colours in all), and gives lots of information about each of the twelve colours. On the reverse, an innovative moving inner wheel, or wheel within a wheel, demonstrates what will happen if another colour is mixed with it. It also demonstrates tints and shades and colour harmonies. This is very useful source of information when mixing and blending fibres, choosing dyes, designing yarn, or doing project work.

COMPLEMENTARY COLOURS

The chemist Michel Chevreul (1786–1889) realized that our perceptions of colour are influenced by the colours that lie nearby or alongside. Towards the end of his life he wrote a treatise to address the problems of dyeing textiles for use in tapestry workshops. In this he argued that although the colours do not change, our visual sensations do, and this can be used to create more vibrancy in a project. The theory was adopted by artists who started to use small dots of complementary colours in their work.

If you are ever in doubt about what colour to add to liven a yarn up or add an accent somewhere in a project, look for the colour's complement, as Chevreul recommended.

Equal quantities of complementary colours in the same project appear stronger when lying side by side, particularly if they cover a large area – something to bear in mind when designing yarn for knitting.

Complementary colours have a strange effect on each other. Side by side the colours can seem to bounce off each other, and small dots can add vibrancy, as Chevreul realized, but blend the two colours together and the result is usually a neutral brown or grey. This 'cancelling out' effect can be used to manage a colour in the same way as tints, tones and shades by reducing the impact of a colour. Conversely, when used as blocks of colour in juxtaposition each colour will stand out more where it appears in the yarn or project.

Complementaries are often added as accents of colour in advertising, in shop windows and on packaging. If something looks a bit dull, then a dash of its complement is a sure and safe way to liven things up. Complementary colours are excellent when contrast is required. When somewhat less impact is needed, they can also be divided into a 'split complementary' – the two colours that lie either side of the complement on the colour wheel.

WARM AND COOL COLOURS

Warm and cool colours make up the two halves of the colour wheel, yellow-green through to orange-red being warm, and red-violet through to blue-green being cool.

As well as the natural affinity some people have with either warm or cool colours, there is a seasonal influence: warm colours evoke thoughts of fire and flame reds for winter; cool colours, such as blue like the sea and sky, feel more summery. In yarn design, cool colours like blue and violet tend to recede while the warm reds and yellows are far more dominant and aggressive.

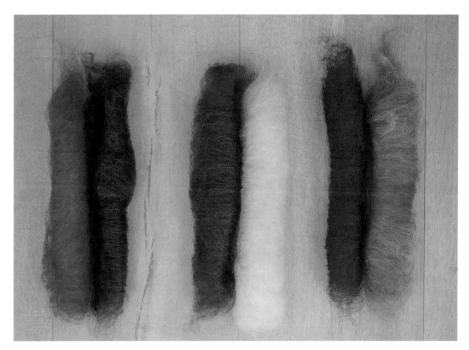

Complementary colours lie opposite to each other on the colour wheel and have an interesting relationship with each other.

When a colour and its complement are blended together in equal measures they cancel each other out.

ANALOGOUS COLOURS

These colours lie next to each other on the wheel and this is a very useful tool for yarn and project design. Colours react differently when three are used together, so, by choosing only colours from within a small section or wedge of the wheel, everything will reliably work together within the project and produce an accomplished looking piece. This is particularly useful for mixed media projects and mixed fibre textural yarns, where silk and mohair, which reflect the light, bring depth and lustre against duller wool, cotton or linen.

THE STRENGTH OF A COLOUR

Previously, we have looked at controlling mechanisms, working within safe places. The next stage is to be a bit more bold, doing something that will make sparks. Have you ever thought of putting orange and bright pink together?

Colours are like people: there are a few extreme characters – some are extrovert and some are introverts – but the majority are in-between. Think of the extrovert as hot yellows, who just cannot be avoided, right there in your face and adding sparkle, wit and firing up everything round about them. Meanwhile, the introverted little violets blend into the background, being quiet, gentle characters, understated and easily missed in a crowd.

Goethe, the renowned poet, was also a colour theorist, and devised a table that helps manage the inherent characteristic strengths of colours when mixing fibre, designing yarn or working with textiles.

Unlike in the dye-pot, coloured, blended fibres never actually get mixed up; they just appear to do so. This appearance is affected by the distance from which you are looking. Try squinting or looking through half-closed eyes to see this effect. It is most significant when compar-

~ INTENSE EARTH ~

~ field ~ Hedgerow ~ Cherry ~ Pasture ~ Ocean ~

leaf ~ sky ~ rust ~ russet ~ pool ~ blush ~ sun

Flint ~ pebble ~ bark

Squint and look at these colours to see which are most powerful.

ing the patterns for say, a scarf or a rug. A fine, delicate pattern for a scarf would be wasted on a rug that would only normally be viewed from several feet away.

Another characteristic of colour is that some colours stand out more than others. Goethe allocated a ratio relative to the strength of each of the primary and secondary colours: violet – 9, blue – 8, red and green – 6, orange – 4, yellow – 3. Orange and yellow are the extroverts and stand out whilst violet disappears into the background.

Interestingly, red and green are given the same weighting (6) so, if you mix the same weight or yardage of red and green in a project, it will give a balanced, even appearance between the red and the green.

The extremes are yellow and violet. Using these two colours together in the same project is a very striking and effec-

tive technique, but it has to be handled carefully, otherwise the yellow takes over and dominates the whole project. (Just as in nature, it is easy to spot the daffodils among the green, but you need to look for the shrinking violets.) To get a balanced effect with these two colours, you would need three times as much violet as yellow, either in weight or volume. When putting colours together, Goethe's ratios offer an invaluable way of predicting outcomes.

AREAS OF COLOUR

The impact of any colour will vary according to the size of the area it occupies. A small yellow dot will show up more than any other dot of the same size. But, whatever colour you are dealing with, it can seem more vibrant when placed alongside tiny dots of its pure complementary col-

our (i.e. the one that lies on the opposite side of the colour wheel).

Particle size need not be seen as a problem. Rather, see it as a useful tool in the toolbox of tricks that textile artists use. If something is to be viewed close up in use, such as a pair of gloves, the colour needs to be handled differently than for, say, a wall hanging, where small particles of colour are invisible when viewed from a distance.

The effect of particle size becomes obvious when blending fibres. Take, for example, equal quantities of red and blue fibre and put them through a drum carder or blend with hand carders. After the first pass the batt will contain small areas of red and blue and some may appear violet where it is well mixed.

When spun, the yarn will have small areas of red and blue and be predominantly the mid-colour.

The effect of particle size and background – violets recede on dark backgrounds while yellows stand out, and a small area of violet appears more blue on a red background.

Card the batt a second time before spinning, and the areas of red and blue will be nowhere near as easy to see.

To do this with hand carders, load one carder with blue on one half and red on the other. The colours will mix as the fibre is stripped from one carder on to the other; the red ends up on top of the blue and blue on the red.

The influence of particle size in project design can be used to create dramatic effects. Imagine you have some lustrous mohair locks dyed in analogous colours of blue-green and yellow. Mixing the locks with a similar weight of dyed fleece, say blue, by putting through the drum carder, will yield a lovely soft yarn when spun and the lustrous blue-green/yellow locks will add halos of texture.

However, if the two were to be spun separately, one bobbin of mohair locks and another of dyed fleece, and then mixed at the plying stage, the locks would catch the light more and make their colour much more obvious. To cash in on this effect, spin the mohair locks as a thick yarn – or perhaps do not spin them at all – and either knit or add into the weaving in blocks, with the spun dyed blue fleece as background.

IN A NUTSHELL

Colour can be anything you want it to be: sumptuous or startling, subtle or soothing. Colour is subjective. If you don't manage colour it can manage you, so be brave, and go with the colours that attract you. Then, if you need to, use proven colour skills and techniques to make colour work for you.

8 Dying to Dye

It is never long in a spinner's life before the right fibre turns up in the wrong colour. The subject of dyeing can be complex if you want it to be: for example, acid dyes only work with animal (protein) fibre; most natural dyes involve the use of chemicals; indigo is a natural dye, but can be synthetic! The plan here is to keep it simple, and the underlying rationale is 'maximum return for minimum skill'.

Think of dyeing like travel: there are so many places to go, and so many different ways of getting there. For the traveller who loves sightseeing, acid dyeing will feel like a very exciting trip with a paintbox into the world of wool and silk dyes. But, to the spinner with their own sheep, who embraces a home-grown lifestyle, nearby dye plants will be a much more fascinating proposition.

Frequently, a spinner will have their own source of fleece or fibre and, understandably, wish to explore colour with their own same fibre. Anyone with lots of white fleece may find dyeing with black or brown a very satisfying first step. Dyeing does not have to involve primary colours.

Alternatively, one may be inspired by something that requires a certain range of colours, or a catalyst sparks off an idea. Sometimes a particular colour is needed to complement an interior design scheme, or accessorize an outfit. There are occasions when one simply wants to spin something to brighten up a dull day, or lift the spirits.

For most spinners, the first dip into dyeing is with commercial acid dyes. These are reasonably easy to acquire and only need vinegar to give predictable, colourfast results. Dyeing with two or more such acid dyes in the same dye pot at the same time is very inspiring and a creative way to explore colour in yarn design. This is particularly true if the basic colour skills described in the previous chapter are borne in mind.

Old kitchen equipment serves well for dyeing, but must never return to kitchen use.

For example, mixing primary colours will reveal some delightful secondary colours; but mixing secondary or impure colours is more likely to yield something resembling mud.

To the enthusiastic and curious spinner who wants to dye anything and everything – preferably right now – then a dip in the indigo vat is the best option. It has to be seen to be believed!

There is something in dyeing to suit every personality. But first a word of warning: like spinning, once you start it can become seriously addictive!

DYE IN THE FIBRE OR YARN?

One of the first practicalities to consider is whether to dye in the fibre, or wait until it is spun into yarn.

Dyeing fibre is a safe option for a beginner, as it offers the chance of redemption, should the outcome not meet expectation. Dyeing hand-spun yarn carries the risk of wasting hours of work if turns to felt or ends up an irredeemable colour. (Felting is usually due to a sudden change of temperature or friction during the dyeing process. It takes friction and heat together to make felt: simmering water is fine, but not boiling, and avoid stirring and poking when the dye bath is hot. Stirring and poking is fine when the dye bath is cold, otherwise resist the temptation, unless you want felt.)

With dyed fibre, there is also the option of manipulating the colour if it is not too dark and can take more dye. Or use the colour skills described in the previous chapter to predict outcomes. Alternatively, the fibre could be blended prior to spinning with more white, neutral or coloured fibre before it is spun.

MAINTAINING COLOUR SEQUENCE

Another colour-related issue is how to accommodate a changing sequence of colours in singles when plying from two different bobbins. One method is to ply with an invisible thread such as polyamide, or bulk nylon. The downside of this is that it is no longer a pure yarn, although it may have other qualities such as additional strength. Another solution is to ply from a single bobbin using the Navajo

technique (*see* Chapter 6). This will result in a final 3-ply yarn which may or may not be acceptable. For this reason dyeing ready spun and plied yarn is often the preferred option, although it is a more complex solution to the problem in terms of dyeing method.

EQUIPMENT

Ideally, dyeing should take place somewhere other than the kitchen. Not everyone has the luxury of a laundry room where smells and mess can be left undisturbed, however. A covered outdoor area or garden shed, or simply outdoors in fine weather, is a convenient and sometimes inspiring option too. Being out of doors is fun and ideal for indigo dyeing, particularly if two or three people are involved. However, it can become messy, even silly, and turn into an indigo party with lasting results.

It is not necessary to purchase special dyeing vessels. An old stainless steel, aluminium or enamel stew pot will serve perfectly well. But, and this is a big 'but', the dye pot must never, ever, be used again for food, as all dyes are toxic to some degree. The same applies to measuring spoons, jars, jugs, ladles, colanders, or any other ex-kitchen equipment.

It is worth buying some plastic measuring spoons, measuring jugs, and some syringes to dedicate to the dyeing equipment box. Scales for weighing fibre are essential and a thermometer will take a little of the uncertainty out of the experience too.

With the exception of indigo, all dyes are toxic to some degree. Some are more toxic than others, and, as allergies seems to become more common, it is a good

Use 100g clean fleece or rovings.

Soak rovings in the dye bath for twenty minutes prior to adding dye.

policy to always play safe, particularly if children or other people are around.

If you are working in the kitchen, cover work surfaces with waterproof material, then with plenty of newspaper or absorbent disposable material. Remove hand towels and tea towels and replace with disposable items. Always wear rubber gloves (skin is absorbent) and an apron, and avoid any risk of inhaling fine particles or steam.

This is not meant to sound frightening, but it is really just common sense. And you will enjoy dyeing much more if you are not worried about making a mess. 'Playing dye' is great fun, but not for unattended children!

A mobile phone seems an odd item to add to the dyer's additional kit list. But, being able to replicate a dye is one of the most useful skills, and photo records can be quick, reliable, and sometimes more accurate than pen and paper. Furthermore, unlike scraps of paper or

notebooks, this valuable information is always to hand and need never be lost – and what is better than to record what something looks like?

RAINBOW DYEING

Dyeing different colours, all in the same pot, all at the same time, is one of the most exhilarating ways to dye fibre for spinning. It is an ideal way to start as very little can go wrong and, as each batch is comparatively small, at 100g in an overall dye session of, say, four or five batches, some pleasant surprises are certain.

It is a good idea to begin with something simple such as this tried-and-tested method. As experience increases so will your daring, and probably so will the odd disaster too! But even the most unpromising output can turn into beautiful yarn in the right circumstances. You just never

know how things will turn out until you try; which is one of the things that makes dyeing such fun. And there is always the option of more dye or blending the fibre before spinning it.

The initial financial outlay is low, requiring only four different dye colours: red, yellow, blue and black. From these colours, it is possible to create almost any other colour.

Acid dyes, such as those from Ashford, which come in small 10g pots and are available throughout world, will dye approximately 100g of fibre with just 1g of dye (i.e.10g will dye 1kg of fibre).

Start with 100g fibre. If this is a commercial roving, it will probably be about 3 or 4 metres long. When spun, 100g will fill an average size bobbin and make a standard skein of yarn.

If you always use 100g for each dye session, it also makes it easy to calculate how much dye to use in future batches. In this way, you will build up a body of

Mix and label dye solutions.

Add dye from syringes in three primary colours.

knowledge more quickly. Dyeing in larger quantities is not appropriate to the rainbow technique as colours will not migrate and merge over large areas.

Measuring 1g of dye is virtually impossible in the average home and it is not necessary to do so. And with the exception of a thermometer and scales for weighing fibre, nor is there any need to purchase any highly specialized equipment for dyeing. The smallest culinary measuring spoon is usually 2.5g so, if you mix this much with 50ml water in a measuring pot, then 10ml from a syringe will deliver about 0.5g of dye.

The actual quantity of liquid or concentration of dye in the dye bath is not critical because it is simply the medium through which the dye is transferred to the fibre. What is important, however, is being able to replicate a dye session. So, don't worry too much about the accuracy of your measuring tools. Just make sure you use the same ones each time and record the measures you use at the time. This way you will build up a body of knowledge and will be able to adjust the dye concentration with each new batch of dye with growing confidence.

DYEING TWO OR THREE COLOURS AT THE SAME TIME

Use a dye pan with about a 10-inch diameter base. Add 1.5 litres cold water, one drop of washing up liquid (this helps with immersion of fibre) and 100ml white vinegar (malt vinegar will work too but has a stronger smell).

Any wool or animal (i.e. protein) fibre or silk will take dye in an acid bath. But fibres of plant origin (i.e. cellulose), such as bamboo, resist acid dye and this can be used to your advantage. Hence, a commercial merino/bamboo mix roving (<10 percent bamboo) is an excellent choice for first-time dyeing, as the cellulose does not take dye and leaves attractive lighter striations of colour running through the merino. This can balance out any areas of intense colour, and lift and enhance those areas where colour is not so strong.

From a practical point of view the bamboo, conveniently, slightly inhibits the tendency of the wool in the whole fibre to felt in the extreme heat of the dyeing process. So, a merino/bamboo mix will offer a practical as well as aesthetically pleasing benefit.

When the dye bath is ready, immerse your 100g dry fibre into the dye bath and leave it to soak for twenty minutes, turning it over at least once to make sure that it is evenly wetted throughout and any air bubbles are removed.

MIXING DYE POWDER

Read carefully the safety directions that come with your dye; these should be securely affixed to the container. Label four old jars – preferably with lids that fit

– Red, Yellow, Blue and Black DYE. Then mix up the four pots of dye with warm water at the concentration described above (2.5g with 50ml water).

Using a syringe, draw up 10ml dye solution from each dye pot. Each syringe can be left sitting in the relevant jar until it is needed and carefully placed back in the same jar after use to avoid colour contamination.

When the fibre in the dye bath is thoroughly soaked, there should still be enough water to just cover the fibre. The volume of water is not critical. If the fibre is not fully submerged, then increase the dye bath using the same acidic value liquid (50ml:1.5l vinegar/water), or remove as necessary. (The acid dye bath is simply the medium through which the dye will travel as it makes its way into the fibre during the heating process. The proportion of concentration of dye in the dye bath is irrelevant. When all the dye has attached to the fibre, the dye bath will become clear again.)

Now add dye to the dye bath. Before doing this, mentally divide up the pan into three equal segments, like a pie-chart. One each to be red, yellow or blue. Then carefully, and very gently, deliver 10ml of dye solution, drop by drop, into each segment of the imaginary pie chart, leaving an area between each where there is no dye at all. Another way to imagine this it to think of it as a clock: put dye between 12 and 18 minutes past the hour; then another colour from 20 minutes past up to 22 minutes to the hour; then the last colour between 20 and 2 minutes to the hour.

Using a smooth stick, or old wooden spoon handle, gently poke the uncoloured areas between each of the primary colours to encourage formation of secondary colours.

Poke to help the colours merge to give secondary colours; then add the black.

Now take 3ml of the black dye syringe and drop some, but not necessarily all of it, evenly over the whole dye bath. This may seem like a strange thing to do, but it is there for a reason: black dye acts like salt, or seasoning in a recipe. You cannot taste salt in a Yorkshire pudding, but you know if it is not there. With dye, a dash of black adds something to the dye batch that is difficult to define, but easy to spot when it is missing. This is also a useful way to modify an unsatisfactory dye batch: just re-dye using a little black and it can transform something garish into something quite sophisticated. Textile artists frequently use a similar technique with colour to make their work more distinctive and easily identifiable as theirs. Spinners can do this too; it is a reason to dye for!

When all the dye is in, gently prod all around the perimeter of the dye pot to encourage dye into all areas, particularly where the colours merge. Agitating the whole dye pot instead of prodding it – as if taking it for a ride in a car – will have a more subtle effect. Too much agitation or prodding will create mud, however, so try to be cautious at the outset and be content to learn by degrees. You can always dye more. And do not prod once the dye bath begins to heat up – no matter how tempting this may be.

SETTING THE DYE

The next stage is to transfer the dye and set it in the fibre with heat. The more slowly the heat is introduced, the more successful the dye transfer will be.

Put the dye pot onto a low heat source and aim to bring it up to simmering point over a period of about 45 minutes. When it reaches simmering, turn down the heat, and maintain simmering temperature for another 30–45 minutes until the dye bath is clear.

Remember that heat and friction together create felt, so be careful not to move the fibre about in the dye bath unnecessarily. To see if the dye has transferred, gently tilt the pan. If the water is clear, then the process is complete and the batch needs to be left to cool for at least another 45 minutes to avoid risk of felting.

When the dye bath is cool, gently remove the fibre, leaving the exhaust liquid in the dye bath for the next batch.

Rinse the fibre in water of the same temperature until it remains clear. Squeeze out as much as possible and dry carefully, away from direct sunlight.

If the roving looks flat and lifeless when it is dry, it can be fluffed out by separating the fibres by hand. Should any felting have occurred, opening up the fibres at this stage will facilitate future carding or fibre preparation before spinning.

To avoid any adverse effect on biological drainage systems, add a teaspoon of bicarbonate of soda to the remaining dye bath before disposing of it down the sink. At the end of the session, if necessary, any leftover dye can be stored (well away from the kitchen!) in the carefully labelled jars, with lids firmly closed. Some dyes keep better than others, and as they are toxic, it is safer to use up the dye rather than store it, if this is possible.

NATURAL DYES

The range of plants for natural dyeing is vast and to explore them here would compromise the purpose of this exercise, which is to give you maximum return from minimal experience. Dyeing does not need to be difficult or complex.

Fibre for natural dyeing, generally, needs to be treated in order to maximize take-up of dye. However, this process, known as mordanting, is not necessary when dyeing with indigo or with walnuts – hence, these two dyes are used for illustration below.

The indigo blue and golden brown walnut colours also go well together, and the raw materials are widely available. There are many, many more plants to dye with, but these two offer maximum return for minimum skill. Keep it simple and enjoy.

INDIGO

Indigo is a dyer's delight. Watching yarn turn from pale yellow/green to dark blue as the air gets to it is an awe-inspiring sight and one does not need a degree in chemistry to be able to produce it.

Indigo (also known as 'woad'; the two are chemically identical) is ideal for dyeing your hand-spun yarn because it needs less immersion time, and a lower temperature, compared to other dye methods. This minimizes the risk of felting.

Because of the impracticality of handling loose fibre, indigo dyeing is also more easily done with skeins of ready spun yarn. The skeins can be suspended from sticks or coat hangers with string loops. The risk of felting is minimal because temperatures do not exceed 70°C. Indigo will dye yarn made of both cellulose and protein fibres. This has profound implications for projects where texture is the main emphasis or other textiles are involved.

Any fibre of animal, plant or synthetic origin, will dye with indigo. Cotton lace, feathers, buttons, bamboo, linen and mohair can all be combined in the same yarn and each textile will accept the indigo dye – as will wooden bobbins, and skin!

The chemical nature of indigo is such that the dye wraps itself around fibre, whereas acid and natural dyeing involves a molecular change or reaction. With indigo, the more dips that take place, the more intense will be the colour as it wraps itself around the target.

It is possible to overdo the dipping: the dye will then flake off in a process known as 'crocking'. But, overall, indigo dye is easy to use and fairly safe. It has antiseptic qualities which was perhaps a reason ancient British warriors reportedly painted themselves with it.

Today, indigo can be of natural or synthetic origin. The natural indigo, though more expensive, has twice the strength of synthetic, but the finished results appear more or less the same.

Indigo dyeing takes place in an alkaline environment, while wool and protein fibres require an acid environment in which to accept dye. The degree of acidity/alkalinity (pH level) can be measured and accurately controlled – or you can just dip in and learn by experience!

One of the reasons indigo dyeing is so popular with hand spinners is that it will dye any fibre to more or less any degree of blue.

Tying or restricting the uptake of indigo in the bath with a *resist* gives interesting effects, as does dyeing a loosely wound ball of yarn, or batch of say, buttons, taffeta, feathers, strips of silk, lace, leather, and other textiles and fabrics that may be used in the final project.

For example, if you were dyeing your first spinning which was not enough for anything larger and of variable thickness, then it could be woven into a cushion along with some of the items above. Even if the original batch of items started off the wrong colour completely, by the time the indigo had done its magical work the whole textile offering would be of a harmonious mix at the very least.

Blue hands last for several days, blue nails even longer!

Indigo will dye any fibre or fabric.

DYEING WITH INDIGO

Dyeing is best done out of doors where possible, as repeated dipping and exposing to the air is, essentially, a messy business. If it must be done indoors, then protection for floors and furniture, as well as clothing and skin, is advisable.

Ingredients

A commercial 'Indigo Dye Kit' is the easy option, although one can buy natural or synthetic indigo, and washing soda and powdered colour-run inhibitor can be found in the laundry section in supermarkets. All raw materials are available from indigo suppliers.

Equipment

Dye pan, bucket or container of 4-litre capacity, thermometer, timer, measuring and mixing spoons, heatproof measuring and mixing jugs, apron, rubber gloves and protection for floors and furniture.

STEP 1   Skeins need to be thoroughly wetted and wrung out before dipping. Dry skeins float on the surface of the dye bath and incorporate oxygen, which reduces efficacy within the dye bath.

STEP 2   Dissolve 50g washing soda in approximately 300ml hand-hot water in a measuring jug and leave to cool slightly. In another small glass jug or jar, mix 1tsp of natural indigo with a little warm water until it is a smooth paste and incorporate this into the measuring jug of hot water.

STEP 3   Stir slowly until the granules have dissolved and can no longer be felt with a spoon crunching (like sugar in coffee) at the bottom of the jug. It is very important that all indigo is dissolved at this stage otherwise it will cause uneven patches of dye in the finished yarn where it settles in the bottom of the dye bath.

STEP 4   Put about 3.5 litres warm water (not exceeding 60°C) into the dye pan and add in the jug of indigo mix, stirring well. For the dye to transfer to the fibre it is necessary to remove the oxygen from the dye bath, which is the purpose of the powdered colour-run inhibitor.

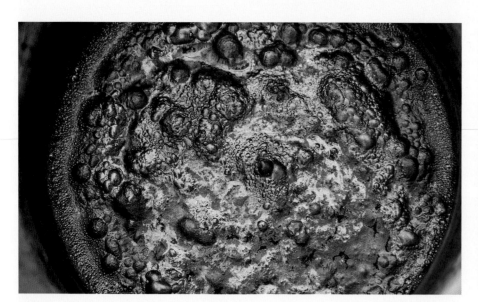

STEP 5   When the indigo mix is thoroughly dissolved in the dye bath, sprinkle 25g powdered colour-run inhibitor over the surface, stir gently to avoid making bubbles, then cover and leave to stand for 30-45 minutes. When the indigo dye bath is ready it will appear iridescent and frothy.

STEP 6   Wearing rubber gloves, unless you want blue hands, gently immerse the wetted skein(s) into the dye bath and move them around gently beneath the surface to encourage an even dispersion and coating of dye. Try to avoid getting air (oxygen) into the liquid as this will make it more difficult for the indigo to attach to the fibre.

STEP 7 The skeins initially turn green.

STEP 8 Leave for 5–10 minutes and then, carefully, remove the skein over the side of the pan without allowing drips to fall back into the pan, as this incorporates oxygen into the dye bath.

STEP 9 As the skein is removed, it appears a greenish colour. Hold the skein over a separate bowl to allow it to drip and watch as the greenish colour oxidizes to give a glorious permanent blue. If the shade is too light, then re-dip, being careful not to introduce air into the dye bath. As the bath is re-used and cools down, the colour will become weaker and take longer to transfer.

STEP 10 Hang the skeins on a washing line to drip and oxidize. It will continue to become a darker blue until the oxidation completes.

STEP 11 When the yarn does not get any more blue, rinse it in warm water to remove any free indigo, or re-dip as required.

Merino/bamboo dyed with black walnuts.

Dyeing with walnuts takes time but is safe and simple.

WALNUTS

'Natural' dyeing yields some very subtle colours and gives a feeling of being at peace with nature: mindful and full of good things. Nothing exemplifies this better than the earth-toned colours extracted from walnuts – anything from a light golden brown to nearly black (the black walnuts illustrated yield a very intense colour). It is difficult to predict because colour outcomes are affected by species, soil quality, source materials such as leaves, hulls, kernels; even the time of harvesting can affect the result.

The species illustrated is from black walnuts gathered from the ground, with hulls, in December. But do not let the absence of a nearby tree be an excuse. There are plenty of walnuts in the shops around Christmas time, and these are a 'win-win', as you can eat the kernels and save the shells for dyeing.

Admittedly, walnut trees are not found in many parks or on street corners, nor are the nuts available all year round. But, when you spot a walnut tree, make a mental note of it. It is an opportunity not to be missed, as even the leaves will dye. And trees don't move! So it is just question of watching and waiting for your moment: the motto, 'to everything there is a season' holds particularly true for natural dyers.

Walnuts will dye straight from the tree but, be warned, they will also dye hands, shoes and anything else they touch.

They have a pleasant acrid smell when raw, but this changes to something less pleasing when it starts to boil! However, the colour walnuts yield is lovely and rich. It can be anything from a divine golden bronze right through to dark brown or even black. It is well worth waiting for and an incredibly straightforward process.

The great bonus of dyeing with walnuts is that it is not necessary to mordant the fibre beforehand (i.e. use a fixing agent). Mordanting can sometimes adversely affect the feel of a fibre.

IN A NUTSHELL

Dyeing can be done with natural or chemical products and does not require specialist skills or equipment. The techniques in this chapter are chosen for ease of use and satisfying results. Just as you do not need to be a mechanic to drive a car, you do not need to be a scientist to dye fleece. As you gather more knowledge and skill, the rewards become greater and more reliable. I hope this chapter will inspire further study.

DYEING WITH WALNUTS

STEP 1   Simply put a panful of nuts, together with any green hulls, in your dye pan and add enough water to cover. The hulls turn black very quickly when they open and are exposed to the air but are perfectly useable.

STEP 2   Cover, and leave the nuts and water to stand overnight.

STEP 3   Next day, bring the pan gently to the boil and simmer for one hour; then leave it to cool down.

STEP 4   When cold, strain the liquor through a colander with muslin or cotton cloth placed inside (the muslin will also become dyed).

STEP 5   Rinse the pan well before returning the strained liquor into it, to avoid fragments transferring to your fibre.

STEP 6   Wet the fibre thoroughly and wring it out before immersing it in the dye bath. (Dry fibre will float on the surface of the dye bath and create an uneven take-up of dye.) Once the wet fibre is immersed, bring the dye batch very gently and slowly up to boiling point, then switch off.

STEP 7   Leave it all to stand overnight again.

STEP 8   Next day, remove the fibre and wash it in wool wash and rinse well to remove any lingering smell.

STEP 9   The dye bath can be carefully labelled and stored for re-use as walnut dye is very strong.

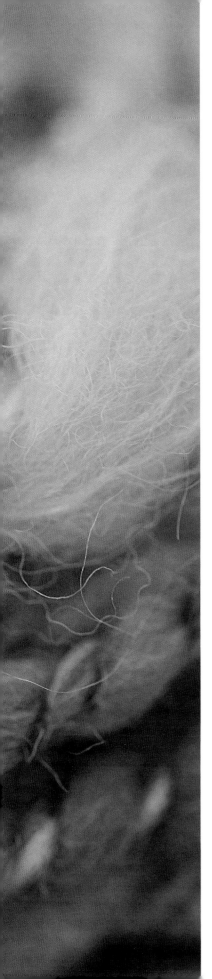

9 Yarn Structure

Yarn structure, that is, the way a spun singles thread is constructed into yarn, dictates the appearance, texture and performance of a yarn. It is one of the four basic elements of yarn design; the other three elements – spinning technique, fibre content and colour – have already been discussed at length. It is probably the most under-used aspect of yarn design, yet it is the easiest of all the spinning skills to take on board. Complete beginners can often replicate a yarn structure even if they can't spin. Any spinner will be able to replicate the classic yarn structures outlined here – and the implications for art, performance, or yarn just spun for the joy of it, are infinite. There is much more to yarn structure than 2-ply!

It is a good idea to practise these yarn styles with waste yarn. This takes the pressure off the learning curve and encourages experimentation; somehow it feels easier to try something new if the outcome doesn't matter.

Think of yarn structure as a broad academic subject like architecture, more concerned with the design and final outcome than with bricks and mortar. House-builders do not lay bricks in an ad hoc manner: there is always architectural input and overseeing. Likewise, spinners always have something in mind when working with fleece; often prompted by fibre or circumstances, they follow a plan (i.e. design their yarn) whether they realize they are doing so or not.

Left to right: 'Lollipop' textured spiral art yarn, 'Greengage Summer' bouclé art yarn, 'Nene-Violet' loose flowing 2-ply art yarn spun on the river, 'Curds and Whey' bouclé art yarn (white Wensleydale), Suri alpaca 2-ply, 'China clay' spiral art yarn (Merino/bamboo/cotton), 'Peach Melba' singles art yarn (merino/acrylic), 'Blue Moon' gimp rainbow-dyed Corriedale.

At first sight, one might expect the chapter on twist and plying to include yarn structure but the two are separate, although related, entities. Twist and plying concern a process in spinning; yarn structure is a permanent design feature of a finished yarn.

Traditional architectural yarn structures include crêpe, bouclé, cable, coil, gimp, spiral, singles, 2-ply and 3-ply, and a whole range of 'variations-on-a-theme' associated with them. Each concerns not the spinning of yarn, but the way singles thread is constructed to make yarn. It can be as simple as putting two Z singles together in the opposite direction, or as complex as creating a yarn with several different layers of fibre surrounding a spun core.

In addition to the classic architectural yarn structures listed above are new structural components that can best be described as technical yarns, which make

other yarn 'do' things. These include techniques like making a yarn always retain its position, so that a garment would always stand away from the body, perhaps, or a trilby would always spring into perfect shape, no matter how it was stored.

There are structural components that make a yarn unbreakable – even by cutting. But why would one want un-cuttable yarn? Perhaps gloves for people who cut their own fingers with secateurs or power tools, or protective clothing for cyclists? Yarn structure is a largely unexplored territory in hand spinning, and can be the most influential aspect of it.

As explained previously, every singles thread needs some sort of structural control in order to make the twist manageable. Without it, spun yarn just becomes a mass of uncontrolled energy. This has always been a problem. We know from archaeological finds that plying was known in Roman times when

it was used in sewing thread, although there is no evidence that yarn was plied for weaving purposes. 'The strength of doubled or plied yarns was appreciated by both Romans and natives.... [It] was the normal practice in the La-Tène period' (J.P. Wild, *Textile Manufacture in the Northern Roman Provinces*).

When it comes to choice of yarn structure, performance and aesthetics can represent opposing poles, and one can come at the expense of the other. Opting for strength and performance can mean losing out on softness and texture. Take, for example, a fisherman's or farmer's hand-knitted pullover, designed to last a working lifetime. The yarn will have been spun fine using worsted technique and several singles plied tightly together to repel wind and water ingress. But the lustrous curly long wool fleece from which the gansey was made, such as a Swaledale or Wensleydale, is unrecognizable, the characteristic lustre and curls of the original fleece sacrificed at the altar of performance. Which is as it needs to be for a garment that needs to sustain life by keeping rain out and body warmth in.

By contrast, the hand spinner, lusting over a luscious Wensleydale fleece, just itching to spin a yarn that looks as if it has just came off the sheep, will want to meet different criteria. A soft, luxurious, curly bouclé pullover would be of little use in extreme conditions, but perfect for the catwalk at the Celebration of Breeds show or public relations event!

As you might expect, the simplest yarn structure is 2-ply, and this has been in use for over 2,000 years – two Z spun singles, plied S. From a structural perspective, two singles plied together can only ever lie side by side. If you ply three singles together, they sit closer together, creating a more dense, round yarn.

To see how this works, place two pencils together, then place three together and compare them end on. Compare how they feel in your hand. You will quickly notice that the triad is, structurally, far more stable than a side-by-side alignment. Add to this the fact that the 3-ply yarn contains a lot more twist in all the singles, and it becomes clear that the difference between the strength of a 3-ply is proportionally greater than that of 2-ply.

BOUCLÉ

Of all classic yarn structures, bouclé is probably the best known. Often thought of as 'bumpy', the word actually derives from the French, meaning 'buckled', as in a candle flame that appears to buckle.

A bouclé yarn structure can fulfill many differing purposes. It can be used to keep or to camouflage, to soften or to strengthen and even enhance the colour and texture of a fibre or fleece. It can give spectacular outcomes for even the most inexperienced spinner and the variations on a bouclé theme are endless.

Of all yarn structures, bouclé is by far the most useful to a spinner wishing to create innovative, artistic and aesthetically pleasing yarn. It can be spun on any wheel, but is easier spun with a jumbo flyer or wheel with a large orifice, and accommodating flyer, as the yarn can be quite thick and fibre sometimes gets caught up on the hooks, particularly in the final, binding stage of spinning.

A bouclé yarn has three structural elements: the core; a wrapping fibre and an outer binding thread. Putting the core and wrapping fibre together (core-spinning), is described in detail in Chapter 3 and repeated here in its relevance to the structure of a true bouclé yarn.

Hand dyed curls ~

Teeswater ~ Cotswold ~ Gotland

~ Leicester Longwool ~

~ Wensleydale Locks ~

The wrapping thread is usually what creates the interest, such as a curly Wensleydale or Gotland; the core does not normally show, and the binder thread holds the whole thing together. From a physical perspective, the start point of a bouclé yarn is a stable core thread (2-ply – S) onto which a fibre roving is wrapped in an S direction. Once wrapped, the core spun element is wrapped again with a binder thread, running in the opposite (Z) direction which completes the bouclé and holds everything in place.

Applying the final binding thread takes out a lot of the twist which was put in when the core thread was wrapped. Hence, the wrapping fibre becomes looser and its natural characteristics more apparent. Also, in this final stage, the internal core is untwisted back to nearer to its original, stable state. Hence the use of a finished, stable yarn for the core. If a singles yarn is used for the core, it is important to make sure it is wrapped in the same direction as spun, otherwise it will disintegrate.

Choose the colour of your core carefully so that it will not stand out should it inadvertently show in the finished yarn.

Hold the core thread under gentle tension.

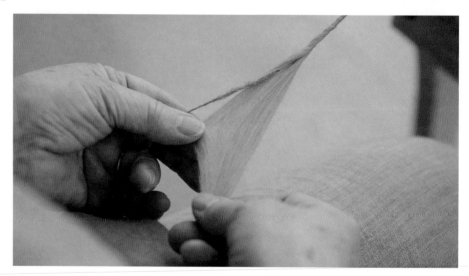

Work with hands close together to increase take up of fibre.

It is helpful to master the technique with an odd ball of finished yarn (normally S plied) and some merino tops or long staple fibre.

Fibre is best drafted into rovings for easy handling, and some silk or sewing machine thread makes a useful binder.

Using leftovers takes the pressure off the learning process. It does not matter if the result is not up to scratch to start with. What matters is getting to grips with the technique. And, like all spinning, once learned, the skill lasts a lifetime. For finished work, it makes sense to choose colours which are 'comfortable' with each other. If the core and wrap are indistinct, then mistakes won't show so much. So a natural core with a natural longwool fleece would work very well.

However, for the purpose of learning this technique, it is helpful if mistakes *do* show up, so, at this early stage, there is an argument for using contrasting colours.

Method

1. Pre-draft the wrapping fibre into a bowl or basket.
2. Place the ball of wool in a basin on the floor on one side (say, left if you are right-handed), so that it does not roll about and get tangled up with the rovings, which are best kept on the opposite side to avoid tangling.
3. Tie the core thread to your leader thread on the bobbin and prepare to spin in the direction that which will increase the twist in the core yarn.
4. Keep the core thread under a gentle tension between your third and fourth fingers of your left hand. Use your other (right) hand to place the fibre rovings alongside the core thread so that as the twist goes into the core. The fibre roving wraps itself around the core thread.
5. Aim to spread the fibres along the length of the core by working with both hands close together, as opposed to holding the rovings out at right angles to the core.

6. If you work with your hands side-by-side it is easier to 'drag' the fibre along the core to increase the take-up with the left thumb and index finger. If the wrap is too thin, then you can go back and apply more – or, preferably, call this a learning curve and keep going in the hopes of doing better! (A common error is for the core to end up covering the fibre roving wrap – when what you want is the opposite! This happens when the tension on the core thread is less than that on the wrapping fibre and the core slips through your fingers and starts to wrap itself around the fibre. It is easily remedied and is only due to inexperience.)

7. Applying the final binder thread is much easier, as it is simply plying. Place your bobbin of wrapped core on the Lazy Kate, along with the reel of thread for binding. This can be silk, which is a good choice for strength, or it could be gold if you're feeling glitzy. Or it could be sewing machine thread if that is all that is available.

8. Remember to turn the wheel in the opposite direction to the previous wrapping stage. Ply the binding thread, altering the tension on it to create more or less definition as required.

Bouclé yarns can be quite bulky so you don't need to spin up huge quantities of yarn for it to be useful. Sections of bouclé make brilliant 'accents' in knitting or in the weft of weaving; they are also useful for knit-weave on the knitting machine. Even a short length of bouclé will add texture and interest to an otherwise uninteresting area in a project.

When designing a project, a section of bouclé can be used to accentuate a colour scheme or fibre type. A long, lustrous fleece such as Wensleydale will lose its lovely curls when carded for spinning. But, if it is spun cut-end to cut-end and the curly tip of lock left unspun this can be used as the wrap for the core. When the binding thread is applied, the fleece will untwist somewhat, leaving the curls more dominant. The result is an incredibly beautiful, as well as totally unique, yarn! It is not necessary to spin a whole fleece this way; just enough to make a design stunning rather than just interesting or unusual.

Although the wrapping fibre is usually dominant, it is easy to create a unique visual effect with an unremarkable roving and a more interesting, possibly ready-made binding yarn, in various or recurring colourways.

Frequently, with bouclé the wrapping thread dominates and it is fibre spinners love, so it makes sense to run off a sample before committing to a whole skein. It is possible to create the slubby sections commonly associated with bouclé by varying the thickness of the chosen fibre at regular intervals. You will find the binder thread will slip over these sections, giving some absolutely delightful features to your unique new yarn.

A woollen core is easier to hold under tension between your fingers than a slippery acrylic or silk, and fibres attach easily to wool. The core does not show, so it seems pointless to spend hours spinning a hand-spun core when you can buy a whole cone of pure wool for comparatively little cost; better to save your efforts for results that show.

There are those who would argue that using bought yarn is 'cheating' and the resulting yarn is not totally hand-spun.

A wool roving will wrap more readily to a fluffy woollen core than a smooth one.

Right or wrong, this is a matter of personal choice. The purpose here is to open up ideas, to explore all the options for spinning beautiful yarn, and to free up spinners' minds from pre-conceived ideas. If using a ready-made yarn turns out to be the springboard for another yarn, does it matter?

CABLE/CORD

When two plied yarns are plied together (in the opposite direction to the first ply), they create something that resembles a cord or rope. This twist combination creates a much stronger yarn than if the same number of singles were plied in the conventional manner – and, of necessity, it is very much thicker. The fibres are tightly bound together and cannot work to the surface easily to cause pilling. The principle is like rope-making and results in an

Cable yarn.

Spun singles from silk slubs and silk rovings ready for coils.

Managing twist is this the most difficult aspect of making coiled yarn. This is because so much twist is needed to make the singles coil around the core. A thick core will create a much more powerful visual effect, but this exacerbates the problem of twist building up in the yarn (due to the inverse relationship between fibre and twist, i.e. more fibre = less twist). To overcome the problem and make a stable coiled yarn, it is necessary to take out the twist inevitably incorporated while making the coil.

The technique of using a drop spindle and wrapping at the same time requires a fair degree of dexterity. It is advisable to learn the technique first, using waste odd balls of commercial yarn rather than your own hand spun. This makes it easier to discard a batch and start again when things go wrong (which they will at first), without feeling guilty about waste.

An electric spinner is ideal for making coils. As well as a large orifice and sliders without hooks, that can catch and tangle, the wheel can be set to turn at a consistently slower speed than most spinners can treadle. And not having to treadle frees up more brain-space – which is useful, as it is necessary to remove twist by means of a drop spindle, at the same time as wrapping the coil. The method is given here, broken down into stages; allow plenty of time, and be patient!

Materials and equipment

- One bobbin of wrapping singles thread for the visible outer coil, placed on a Lazy Kate to the right of the spinner (if right handed).
- One lightweight top whorl drop spindle loaded with a length of thick core thread, preferably wool (this will grip the coils more easily than a core of smooth slippery fibre).

exceptionally strong yarn. When knitted, a cable or cord yarn makes stitches that are more clearly visible than conventional 2- or 3-ply. A 3-ply cable works well because the strands can lie close together, creating a tighter bond. The Navajo ply technique is ideal; however, the drawback to this is that the cable is much thicker than if it were 2-plied. For project work and short lengths the cable can be very striking.

COILS

Coils are made from a decorative Z-spun singles wrapped around a thick core (invisible in the finished yarn), and are ideal for jewellery making or couching. It is neither necessary nor appropriate to make large quantities of coils. Carefully chosen blends of colour and fibre combinations for the outer visible coil give spectacular results when viewed closely packed together.

Practise rolling the core from fingertips towards the palm.

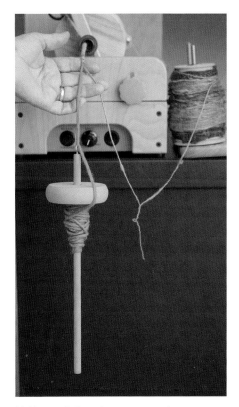
Making coils is easier on an e-spinner.

Method

1. Connect the core from the hook of the top whorl spindle through the orifice, sliders or hooks and onto the bobbin.

2. Set the wheel to turn Z. Hold the core thread in your left hand, palm upwards, letting the spindle hang between your knees. This is another reason to avoid having to treadle.

3. Switch on, turning forwards, or Z direction (as if spinning), and, as the twist enters the core, allow the core to untwist itself by rolling it across the palm of your hand toward the fingertips. This will set the spindle turning as the new twist exits. There is no need to set the spindle spinning or worry about spin direction of the spindle, as it will sort itself out.

4. As twist builds up in the core, it will naturally exit via the free moving spindle. When the twist is released and the wrapped thread stable, allow the core to store on the bobbin. A lightweight spindle requires less Scotch tension for winding onto the bobbin. The gravitational pull of a heavy spindle will draw the wrapped yarn back out through the orifice so this is best avoided.

5. Now, start a new section and, as the twist builds up, roll the core back from the fingertips over the palm to encourage the twist to exit via the spindle.

6. Store each small section on the bobbin when it is wrapped and any extra twist (used to make the wrap) has been expelled through the drop spindle, and the completed coiled yarn is stable.

Practice session

Take time to become proficient at rolling the core from your fingertips across your palm without using your other (right) hand – you will need your right hand later for controlling the coils. After a time, you will feel a rhythm developing and you can adjust the speed until it is comfortable and easily manageable. You can encourage the twist to move in the right direction by rolling it down the little finger of your right hand and onto the fingertips of your left hand. (This sounds much more difficult than it is in practice.)

Do not bother with the wrap at this stage; just twist and untwist short lengths of the core, storing them on the bobbin as each length is restored to its original balance.

You will need to stop every so often to release a new length of core from your drop spindle. Take the opportunity to

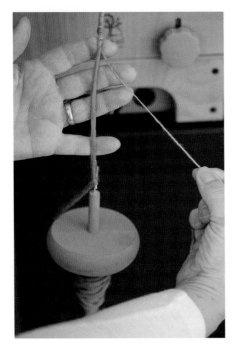

When you can handle twist going in and out through the spindle, it is time to start coiling the singles onto the core – this is the easy part.

Coils yarn, hand dyed.

examine the core that has been wrapped onto the bobbin to see if any unwanted twist remains in it. Aim to have no more twist on the section of core thread on the bobbin than there is on the drop spindle.

The aim of this practice session is to be able to start with, and finish with, a balanced yarn. Once you can achieve this balance of putting twist in and allowing the same amount back out again through the drop spindle, the most difficult part of the learning process is over.

Once you are proficient then it is time to relax and enjoy the next stage as wrapping the core is a far more simple and straightforward manoeuvre than learning to control the spindle and wheel or e-spinner at the same time.

- Take the singles from the bobbin on the Lazy Kate and attach with a knot to the core thread.
- Start the forward clockwise twist and holding the singles in your right hand, carefully and slowly allow it to wrap, evenly, over the core, completely covering it as you go. As you do this, twist will build up in the core in your left hand, so take out the twist by rolling it from fingertips down your hand which appears as S, reverse, or anticlockwise twist in the drop spindle.

It is quite acceptable to wrap a section and then remove the twist from it in two separate movements. You will soon find you have achieved the dexterity to do both at the same time and then the drop spindle will gather its own momentum.

If the finished coils contain more twist then planned, then twist them even more and ply them into a really thick yarn using the Navajo or Andean technique (*see* Chapter 6). This will make a thicker and even more spectacular yarn. Any attempt to untwist the yarn, at this later stage, will loosen the wrapped coil away from the core and spoil the effect. By plying, in this way, you will be using one yarn structure to manage the twist in another – which is what this chapter is all about.

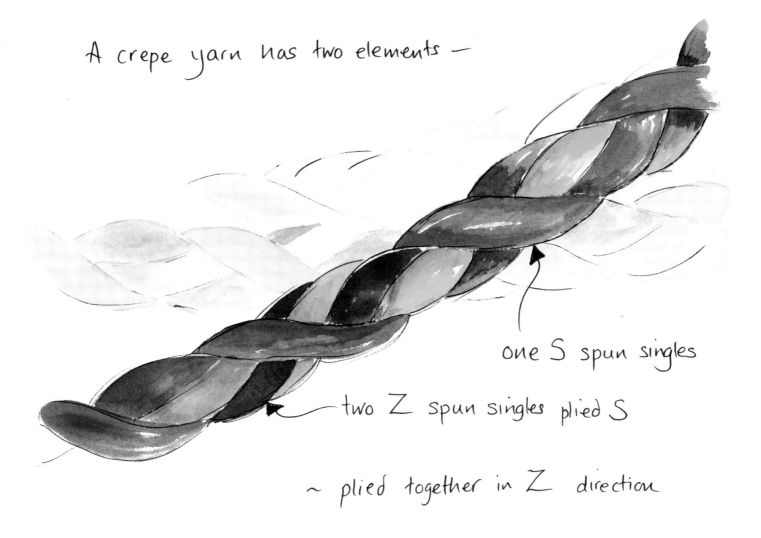

A crepe yarn has two elements —

one S spun singles

two Z spun singles plied S

~ plied together in Z direction

CRÊPE

A crêpe yarn is a triad of singles, so looks and feels rather like a cord but with a more bumpy-loooking texture. It can be used to great effect when using different coloured singles spun to different thicknesses.

It takes three singles to make a crêpe; two are spun S, and a third spun in the traditional Z direction.

1. First, ply together the two S-spun singles in Z direction with double the amount of twist you would normally use.
2. Now, ply this high-twist Z 2-ply with your remaining Z-spun singles in S direction.

Take care to hold the tension, equally, during the final ply, as the 2-ply will be full of energy as it comes off the bobbin. Crêpe yarns make clear stitch definition and look good when laid-in on machine knitted fabric. Plying crepes, using a commercial Z-spun novelty yarn of similar thickness, makes for some very interesting and unusual spinning!

GIMP

A gimp yarn comprises two single threads, one of which is twice the thickness of the other.

1. Spin one bobbin of thick singles in Z direction with plenty of twist.
2. Now, spin half a bobbin of singles in the same direction but half the thickness and, again, plenty of twist.
3. Ply these together in S direction with even tension on both singles and you will have a gimp yarn. The thinner singles appears to cut into the thicker one and this effect can be maximized by subtle colour combinations and has interesting outcomes in knitting.

SINGLES

Commercial manufacturers use chemicals and heat to set twist in singles yarn and to modify the physical structure of wool so that it does not shrink or felt when laundered – an option not open to spinners. However, we do have other, less invasive options such as starch and felting, which will stabilize twist in a singles.

Spinning big fat chunky singles feels like a fibre feast when working with colour. Because it is not plied, colour changes and sequences do not get mixed up. It looks spectacular, particularly when incorporated with novelty yarn and it is quick and easy to produce. Most of the work is done beforehand preparing the fibre roving; the spinning is simply worsted draw and putting in twist, as necessary.

1. Start with a roving. This can be a single colour, but hand dyeing in rainbow or harmonious colours gives a spectacular outcome.
2. Split the roving lengthwise into manageable lengths and draft each length out into a longer, even, roving.
3. Spin the roving using worsted draw, keeping it of even thickness; a roving that is carefully drafted in the first instance makes this more simple and the worsted spin resists pilling and will wear better than a woollen long draw. An even draft will avoid twist building up in thin places, and leaving the thick places without enough twist (remember that twist, unavoidably, migrates to places where the yarn is thin).
4. Adding a decorative commercial yarn at the spinning stage, possibly in a complementary or analogous colour, will enhance an otherwise uninspiring coloured roving. You may already have some suitable thread in a sewing box that will add interest and help with the inherent problem of instability.

Singles is quick to produce but managing twist in singles is the drawback, as it is very unstable once off the bobbin. Call it 'energized', if you wish, but the fact remains that singles yarn will snarl up into a tangled mass, the minute it gets the chance. Even if wound into a tight ball, it is unsuitable for standard knitting or crochet; it can be used as weft in weaving, however. Knit with unfinished singles where the twist is not set, and the knitted fabric will slant one way or the other, depending on the direction of twist.

Industrial processes used to stabilize singles involve chemical treatments and heat – sometimes by passing thread swiftly through a flame. Fortunately, the options available to the hand spinner are kinder to the fibre, and less hazardous to the spinner!

There are two ways of 'finishing' or setting the twist in singles to make it into a stable yarn suitable for knitting, weaving or crochet. It can either be slightly felted, which permanently sets the twist, or, treated with starch or size.

First, skein the singles on a Niddy-Noddy or skeiner and tie very loosely in a figure-of-eight knot in three or four places.

Felting

To felt a skein of singles:

1. Dunk the skein in a bowl of hand-hot soapy water and manipulate it until you can feel it felting.
2. Rapidly increasing or decreasing the water temperature will encourage felting to take place.

Felting takes place when heat and friction cause the microscopic scales of woollen fibres to open up and then lock into each other. Once felting takes place, it cannot be undone, so proceed carefully as only a little is necessary to set the twist. Fortunately, the felting process is progressive and starts slowly so it is just a case of being watchful.

Some fleece will felt more easily than others. Start carefully with hand-hot water but, if this doesn't work, then increase either the heat, or the friction. But do it slowly, as too much felting will spoil the texture and stick the strands together (if this happens, they can usually be pulled apart, so all may not be lost). Should the singles be reluctant to felt, then the temperature of the water can be increased and the yarn dunked, using tongs. Dipping into really hot water then straight into cold water seems to 'shock' the fibre into felting.

It is worth remembering that dyeing can also create slight felting, so if you plan to dye, then leaving it until later may be a smart move.

Hang up the skein to dry and apply a little weight – such as a plastic bottle which can be tied on by the handle and partly filled with water to increase weight as necessary.

Sizing

Alternatively, the skein can be treated ('sized') with xanthan gum. This is a gluten-free food additive that has the effect of sticking the fibres together and thus setting the twist. It is cheap to buy and can be found on the gluten-free shelves in most supermarkets. Unfortunately, this is only a partial or temporary solution as the size is water soluble and washes out in use. But it has the effect of stabilizing the yarn so that it can be used.

When a final work is washed, the size is washed out. This may free up any remaining energy in the yarn and will either cause havoc or be a pleasant surprise. Either way, it will be a permanent and largely unpredictable effect, but there is plenty of opportunity here to create a unique piece of work by using this effect to advantage.

For example, you could weave a large scarf, leaving gaps and changes in the weft sequence as you go, and wait for the energy to do its work and make striking textural effects as the size is washed out. The result will be likely be both pleasing to the eye and technically impossible to replicate. Any shrinkage will have no detrimental effect on, say, a scarf. And it will be totally unique.

Method

1. Soak the skein in a bowl of warm water.
2. Dissolve 2 tsp of xanthan gum in a blender or mug of cold water, whisking with a fork to dissolve any lumps (lumps will dissolve naturally, given time).
3. Squeeze out the skein and drain off the water.
4. Add the gum and work it into the yarn with your fingers.

5. When the gum is worked in as much as the skein will take, lift out the skein with one hand, drawing off excess as you go.
6. Loosen any threads that are sticking together and hang to dry, weighted with a mug or cup tied to the bottom to help straighten the yarn.
7. Turn and separate threads during the drying process to even out the point of pressure at which it is suspended.
8. Should the skein dry in a solid mass, then simply dunk the skein briefly in water to loosen the binding agent, and hang again, freeing up the threads periodically as they dry.

Fat singles is much easier to spin and also easier to finish by felting or sizing than thin yarn. Twist is what causes the problem and the inverse relationship between fibre and twist means that the thicker the fibre, the less twist it needs; therefore, the less twist there is to cause trouble. Also, there is little point in going to all the work of spinning singles if you can hardly see the difference. So spin fat for impact.

By its nature, a fat singles thread will have less twist and, sadly, may not wear as well as a 2- or 3-ply made from the same singles. It is also far more likely to pill as the looser fibres can work their way more easily to the surface and clog together making those annoying little bobbles.

On the up side, however, the singles colour will be more obvious on a fat singles thread because larger areas of colour show up more than small ones (*see* Chapter 7). And remember that a singles yarn will maintain a colour sequence without any adjacent colours becoming mixed up. Making unique singles has many attractions, once you get all that energy going the way you want.

SPIRALS

A spiral yarn comprises two elements, one of which appears to wrap around the other. Choose a fine and a bulky yarn for the spiral; fine silk is a good choice, as its light refracting properties are enhanced where the duller, bulky thread appears to weave around it. This is achieved by holding the thinner element under more tension so that it travels a straighter path while the second element wraps around, creating a spiral effect.

At first sight, it is easy to confuse a spiral yarn with a 2-ply, but the two are quite different. 2-ply is a balanced mix of two singles which are both held under the same tension and are equal partners in size, shape and influence; the components lie side by side and one does not wind around the other as occurs in a spiral yarn.

Making a spiral yarn requires the same technique as applying the binding thread to a bouclé yarn described earlier in this chapter. The bulky wrapped core of the bouclé forms one bobbin, and a finer bobbin of hand-spun yarn or cone of decorative commercial yarn, lurex, cotton, or bulk nylon could form the other element.

Method

1. Place two bobbins on Lazy Kates, preferably one to the right and one to the left so that each thread does not get tangled.
2. Assuming the singles to be plied are traditionally spun Z, turn the wheel anticlockwise for plying – S direction. The position of the hands and tension on each thread is critical in making spirals: any variation by, say, moving the hands further apart, altering the angle of feed or changing grip, will have a dramatic effect on the spiral.

Spiral yarn, hand dyed.

3. Connect both singles to the leader thread at the orifice. Hold the thinner thread between finger and thumb for plying and place so that the thread lies between the second and third, and then the third and fourth (little) fingers as it travels from the Lazy Kate in order to set and help maintain an even tension during plying. Hold the thicker thread in the other hand between finger and thumb so that it is free from tension.

4. Now, bring the hands together so that your middle fingers are in contact with each other. Keeping this contact will ensure that the spiral stays even; if the hands are moved further apart the spirals will form too closely to make the desired spiral effect. Almost any singles of differing thickness can be used to make unique spiral yarns.

YARNS THAT 'DO' THINGS

There is a little-known range of specialized technical commercial yarns available to hand spinners in small quantities, which can best be described as 'yarns that do things'. These can be incorporated into a hand-spun yarn in order to achieve some unusual effects. Elastic is an obvious technical yarn, but how about something that will make your hand-spun yarn glow the dark? Or a yarn that will make your yarn stay in exactly the shape to which it is moulded?

Or, think about the implications for a yarn additive that will ensure a fabric will always return to a particular size or shape, no matter how much it is pulled or stretched.

There are yarns that are invisible but will add strength or elasticity, or both. Some will add so much strength that it is impossible even to cut them with a knife. Useful if you are knitting protective gloves for gardeners or cyclists, perhaps? In complete contrast are coned commercial yarns such as fine mohair and silk which will tone down an over-bright colour, and add a mystical cloud-like aura.

For more ideas or information on technical yarns visit Uppingham Yarns (www.wools.co.uk) – a unique family business which supplies a wide range of unusual commercial and technical yarns, samples and ends-of-line in small quantities, for machine knitters, weavers, spinners and textile artists.

IN A NUTSHELL

Classic yarn structures support an infinite range of art, utility and performance yarns. Learning how to create the classic yarns is far easier than learning to spin, but relatively few spinners take the trouble to learn. In spite of its major impact on the performance, appearance and texture, yarn structure is the most under-used of all the elements of yarn design, other aspects of which include spinning method, fibre, and colour.

10 Mindfulness and Art

Spinning should lift the spirits, and bring joy, meaning and satisfaction. Every spinner is a uniquely creative being in the making, capable of bringing something much more than just '2-ply' into the world. The rationale of the previous chapters was to enable spinners to become independent and discerning about how and what they spin; the next stage is to find and develop a uniquely personal style that leads to the pleasure, satisfaction and fulfilment that becoming a hand spinner brings.

Ask yourself: 'Does what I am doing bring me joy?' If not – if your spinning is a monotonous treadmill – then maybe it's time to change. Time to get off the treadmill and into action, with the confidence that whatever happens you will be the wiser for it, and it could well turn out to be your best spinning so far.

Knowledge and ability gives you the power to decide what is going to happen, but vision and determination are also required. I hope there is enough help and inspiration in these pages to bring about the spark that enables you to take control, and start to become the spinner you were always meant to be. It is a process that continues throughout life. It could be: 'I am going to bring yarn into being that has not been there before … this yarn will be entirely from my own choice, regardless of convention … I am going to spin yarn that means something to me… I will make yarn that reminds me of my holiday, or that tells its own story, or that is mindful of the earth's resources.'

In other words, now that you have the skills, you can decide what happens, take control and spin something meaningful. Think of it like being in charge of an army: you know how to do the job, what men and resources you've got and what they are capable of, and how they will behave in given circumstances. It is just the same with fleece… except that here you can afford to take a risk or two! Do not be constrained

Shetland hap in Shetland wool (by E. Canfield), being 'dressed' by stretching on a wall mounted frame and, below (folded on table) finished hap in Blue-faced Leicester and mohair (by P. Austin).

Isle of Skye Weave (2016), in acrylic and hand-spun yarn by M. Spacey.

Isle of Skye May (1996), inspiration for *Weave.*

with ideas can be easily acquired – students of design do it all the time. Learn the basic steps in the design pathway, and it will rapidly alter one's perception of things – as well as the perception of the self as 'creative'.

The written word is a poor tool with which to convey something as emotive, inspirational, and spiritually uplifting as spinning. Examples are better.

Take the Shetland hap, for instance. On one level it was a simple wrap women crofters made to keep themselves warm in the wet and windy Shetland Isles. But look at it again: think about it, see the symbolism, note the skill that went into spinning and knitting. Imagine how these people must have lived. The simple wrap is actually a recognized heritage piece, and a work of art. The *Old Shale* pattern is reminiscent of waves on a beach, the peaked edges like snow-covered hilltops. The naturally varying colours of Shetland fleece imitate frothy waves and the warm lofty nature of the spun yarn allows it to stretch and tie round the waist.

So, on a visual level the Shetland hap connects us with the landscape with its unique structure, shape, colour and texture. On a spiritual level it makes connections with what we know of how hard life on the Shetland Islands must be.

Structure, form or shape, colour and texture are the very concepts today's students of design use to extract visual cues from their Pinterest pages and mood boards. Hand-spun yarn also has its own unique structure, form, colour and texture. These things go together. The variations on a theme of fleece or fibre, spinning technique, dyeing, plying method and yarn construction are endless. How can a spinner, with even basic knowledge of the concepts discussed in previous chapters think themselves 'not very

by the opinion of others – that way lies monotony. Instead, take what you have learned so far and run with it.

Many spinners say, 'I'm not very creative', which reveals more about self-awareness than actuality. Spinners cannot spin unless they are creative and have the idea to spin in the first place; what is miss-

ing is usually confidence and inspiration. Creativity is making connections between concepts and reality – most people do this all the time without being aware of it. An idea comes to mind but it does not come out of nowhere at all. There is always a catalyst. Something sparks it off. The skill of making connections and coming up

A project book of pleasant images from past events can provide inspiration in the future.

creative'? It can't be true, not for anyone who has the skills of a spinner!

All spinning can represent values, perceptions and ideas sparked off by connections between the individual world we inhabit, and the world of fleece and fibre. Every yarn or project can tell its own story. Give spinning meaning and purpose, and it will bring you joy. The choice is there, and the catalysts for inspiration are everywhere, just waiting to be used.

BE INSPIRED

Start by collecting together a few things you like – drawings, photographs, birthday cards, fabric and yarn samples, leaves, beads, wrapping paper, old travel and sales brochures, gardening, hobbies, homes and interiors magazines, anything you like.

Try not to think about it. Just gather things together, along with spray glue, split pins, sticky tape and some large pieces of card. Allow yourself time and

space to just 'be' and mess about; cut and paste the bits and pieces onto the cardboard, arranged as they happen. Don't plan: just do it. Leave gaps or overlay the images or fabrics in any way that pleases you. The more childlike and carefree you can be, the better.

If the first board doesn't please you, then start another – it doesn't matter. Like spinning, no-one wrote the rule book – you do as you like. Just get things together on a large sheet of card or board, or if it feels more comfortable stick them in a scrapbook.

The next stage in the design pathway is to extract cues from the collection of things on your board or scrapbook. These can be colours, shapes, structure, textures and emotive words.

Colour is one of the easiest things to use as your inspiration. You don't need to be an accomplished artist with expensive paints – just call in at the DIY shop, pick up some free paint shade cards, and you will have all the colours you need for free. Match the samples with colours that appear on the board and cut and paste

them onto smaller pieces of card. Arrange into harmonious families (*see* Chapter 7) or analogous groups. Maybe, add dots of complementary colours that appear in fabric form on your board. Make holes in the colour cards, and use split pins to attach them to your board at appropriate places. The cards can swivel and reveal what is underneath, possibly triggering other combinations you might not have considered.

You can also identify and extract structures: what lines are on your board? Are they mostly zig-zags, wavy lines, horizontal lines or vertical? Are the shapes generally angular with squared-off sides, or rounded like petals?

To extract textures, imagine you could not see, but had to identify the things on your board by feeling them. Would they be smooth, soft, prickly, rough, sharp, bumpy, silky?

What words would you use to describe your board to a blind person? Chances are your board will elicit an overall feeling of something or other: zig-zags, points, squares, vertical lines, sharp clear-cut

Subtle colour and refracted light shown in this mood board are reflected in hand-spun yarn by V. Kemp.

edges in striking colours indicate words like 'exciting', 'stimulating', 'fizzy' and 'vibrant'. Write words anywhere on the board just as they come into your head; this will help to connect with, or reinforce, an emotional response. If the board appears quiet and calm with wavy horizontal lines, subtle colours and soft textures, then words like 'peace', 'pastoral', 'sleepy', 'smooth and sensuous' might spring to mind. Or, maybe, words like 'quirky', 'quizzical' or 'quixotic' will pop up in your head. Whatever it is, don't judge, just write it down without thinking about it, as this is an integral part of the design process.

Next, get out or think about the fleece and fibre or collection of bits and pieces you have in your stash, or have seen and are lusting after and just longing for an excuse to buy. What about the dyed tops that were not what you expected? The sari silk you don't know what to do with? The pilled pullover that could be dyed and unpicked?

The more you ponder and play about with these things, somewhere, somehow and, in some indefinable way, one or more of them will connect with something that is on your board. Something springs to mind or just feels worth exploring. In the case of the mood board, the spark of an idea translated from sparkling glassware into grey, and dark green and purple sparkly yarns.

Just as a compass needle always comes back to pointing the same direction, you will feel a personal response like a sort of magnetism that draws you one way or another. Just go with the flow of it, and ask yourself, 'If my board were music, would it be a waltz – or heavy rock? Would it be like the 1812 Overture complete with canons going off? Or like a sweet song from the Auvergne?'

Explore the 'what-ifs'. What if I put this (fibre/fleece/recycled yarn) with that (colour) which reminds me of this (shape/image/place/thing) on my board. What would the purpose of my yarn be? At this point the four elements of yarn design – spinning method, fibre, colour, yarn structure – come into focus. So what spinning method should I use? What yarn structure will give me the look or performance? What colours match the 'feeling'? Does it suggest a knit pattern or stitch

perhaps? Zig-zags, bumpy moss stitch, cables or fluff?

The design process is seldom a 'eureka' moment. More often, it is a gradual development, a process by which something evolves as a result of the connection of discrete or disparate ideas – and, possibly, of emotive endeavour. Like any process, it can move quickly or slowly. The journey might feel all 'stop and start', or you might just sail through like a ship with the wind in its sails.

Let's take the worst case scenario, however: you've been all day with scissors and glue, and the only thing your mood board has given you is a bad mood! You've wasted all that time trying to be a designer – process, structure, colour, form, texture – and not a glimmer of inspiration to show for it You must therefore be the only spinner in the world without a creative bone in your body. No: all spinners are creative, they create yarn! Maybe you were intimidated by the idea of a mood board and out of your comfort zone. It would not be surprising if you were, and in such circumstances you would be unlikely to make intuitive connections and be inspired. But all is not lost. Try this…

USE YOUR PROJECT BOOK OR MOOD BOARD FOR A QUICK FIX

For the purpose of this exercise, just imagine your project scrapbook or mood board includes a photograph of a sunset over the Bay of Naples (or whatever postcard or picture you choose). Go to your stash and pick out about 80–100g of fibre in the same colours as in the photo (or go online to World of Wool and order it).

Does it need a bit of light, sparkle or gradations of colour, somewhere? How about adding some silk, or a few scraps of Angelina fibre? Assemble the fibres into rough gradations of colour and make up two matching stacks of rolags (*see* Chapter 5).

Gradually use up the colours and make the two stacks at the same time, five for one, five for the other stack. Build up the layers, placing five rolags one way, then the next five at right angles so they are cross-wise and will stack up without rolling off.

If necessary refer back to the chapter on colour skills for ideas about how to lighten, darken, strengthen or soften and change colours. As the stacks grow you will see the effect of the colours and can compare it to your picture.

Hopefully you will soon have something to spin that looks a bit like sunset over the Bay of Naples. Spin up the rolags, using a long draw to allow the fibres to attenuate naturally and add plenty of twist. Spin two bobbins of a consistent singles. Enjoy the colours of the changing sunset as you go. Spinning with colour never fails to lift the spirits.

And then come more options: to ply or not to ply; 2-ply or Navajo ply? Or ply with something that will do something to the yarn (make it stronger, glow in the dark, shimmer, give it a halo of mohair). Does it need texture? If so, consider one of the classic yarn structures described in the previous chapter.

Maybe now would be a good time to revisit your mood board. It might suggest something other than a bad mood this time! It is easy to be intimidated by something new, particularly as one gets older. Confidence can rapidly disappear as we often imagine things to be far more difficult and complex than they are. Dealing with conceptual and concrete things at the same time is not easy, which is where the mood board serves a purpose. It helps

Sunset rolags in merino/bamboo mix, rainbow dyed with fine gold Angelina fibre.

one to make connections between a collection of 'things' and leads to other ideas.

Sunset over the Bay of Naples inspired your sunset-coloured, light-refracting fibre collection, which inspired you to spin your sunset yarn. Now what? What use might you put it to? Are you going to keep this uniquely personal yarn just for the joy of it? Could there be a greater purpose for what you have brought into being? Would it mean something to someone else? How about a return visit to that old mood board? Things are nearly always different the second time around.

USING YOUR HAND-SPUN YARN

SOCK YARN

Sock yarn has demands made of it that other yarns seldom experience (pressure, heat, sweat, to name a few), and for these

reasons 100 percent wool is not always the best choice. There is no joy to be found in spending hours and hours spinning and knitting a pair of socks only to find your toes peeping through on the first wearing.

If you ply a bobbin of worsted spun merino or quality wool with a bobbin of hand spun or commercial silk or even bulk nylon/polyester thread you will have a high performance sock yarn.

A tight worsted spin increases strength but it comes at the expense of being comfortable, springy and soft to the skin of your feet. Using mainly wool and adding a manmade fibre, usually less than 20 percent, is a good compromise, as it improves performance without any appreciable loss of texture or absorbent quality. A silky and lustrous long wool can be very slippery underfoot and not comfortable to wear, and it will quickly felt as a result of the movement.

Choose the colour of any additional ply or fibre carefully, remembering the influence of colour that might reflect the wear-

'Meadow socks'. Socks make lovely gifts, but the yarn must be spun to withstand the extreme pressure of being trodden underfoot and repeatedly stretched at the toes and heels against the lining of a shoe.

Shetland haps become heirlooms.

er's personal style. Bear in mind which colours stand out and which retreat. You will soon have a sock yarn and be faced with more choices: whether to knit identical twin socks (well, nearly), or sibling socks that look as if they belong together but are a bit different, for example.

Your socks will be meaningful if they were inspired by a picture of a wildflower meadow or sunset recorded on your mood board or in a project book. You will always think of them as your 'meadow' or 'sunset' socks. The mood board will have served its purpose.

If knitting socks is a skill too far, then maybe a cushion cover or scarf would be more realistic. But don't just start at one end and plod on to the other. Look at the textures, shapes and structures on your board; can you build them into your project with some fancy stitch work or knit some holes (yarn over, knit two together)? If you start in the middle and knit to the end with one skein, then you could, perhaps, pick up the stitches in the middle and knit up the other skein, for a balanced project. Or maybe knit diagonally as described in the centre section of the shetland hap below.

SHETLAND HAP – A PROJECT THAT MEANS SOMETHING

Your first inspired creation probably won't be something as unique and outstanding as a Shetland hap. But, should those lovely wavy lines that remind you of the seashore inspire you, then copy the idea. No-one owns the patent on haps and the wavy lines are sensational.

The pattern is very striking and meaningful, but not as difficult as it looks. The stitches required are plain, purl, yarn over, and knit two together. You will still be making a project that 'tells a story' and it will probably become a family heirloom as well.

To spin the yarn choose a quality Shetland fleece, prepare and spin long draw either from rolags or combed fleece – whichever you find easier. Spin a 2-ply yarn that will wrap around a ruler about twelve times per inch. It is better over-plied than under, as the shawl is stretched a lot during the dressing and finishing process. The precise number of wraps per inch is not critical as long as the knitting needle size is appropriate to the width, i.e. it will give a soft, loose fabric in garter stitch, which will tolerate stretching and blocking.

Traditionally, these were everyday items worn in the Shetland Islands. The wavy section (Old Shale pattern) represented waves breaking on a beach and the peaks around the edge are said to be reminiscent of snow-capped hills. The yarn needs to be stretchy which is true of Shetland fleece and any fleece that has a natural crimp and is spun long draw. Although not traditional, modern detachable cable needles of the type made by KnitPro are essential for the pattern described here.

Within the Shetland breed there are nearly thirty different registered colours to choose from. A centre colour, say natural white, two other darker colours for the Old Shale section, and peaks in the same colour as the centre works well. Proportionately this means you will need two or three times as much yarn of the centre colour as the other two.

The Shetland hap is designed for Shetland fleece and nothing works as well, but Shetland fleece is not essential. Blue-faced Leicester works well although it has a different, less stretchy texture when finished. Another variation is to spin a singles in Shetland and ply this with a fine commercially spun silk/mohair.

The centre section is knitted back and forth. The next, wavy, section is knitted in the round using needles with detachable cables and the outer peaks are knitted back and forth picking up one stitch at a time from the Old Shale edge.

Start with about 5mm needles and increase the size as necessary, to maintain a soft, open fabric throughout.

Once completed, the shawl is washed and stretched on a frame, as illustrated, or it can be blocked on a bed or carpeted floor. It is not until this point that the outstanding beauty of the shawl becomes apparent. During knitting, the shawl appears fairly small and insignificant – rather like a fluffy cygnet before it matures into an elegant and awe-inspiring swan.

The centre section

- Cast on 3 sts
- Row 1: yarn over (YO) and knit to end for 18 rows = **21sts**
- Knit a row of holes: YO knit two sts together (K2tog), throughout the row. *This indicates where the block of Old Shale 18 sts pattern repeats*
- Yarn over (YO) and knit to end for next 18 rows = **39 sts**
- Knit a row of holes (YO K2tog)
- Yarn over (YO) and knit to end for next 18 rows = **57 sts**
- Knit a row of holes (YO K2tog)
- Yarn over (YO) and knit to end for next 18 rows = **75 sts**
- Knit a row of holes (YO K2tog)
- Yarn over (YO) and knit to end for next 18 rows = **93 sts**
- Knit a row of holes (YO K2tog)
- Yarn over (YO) and knit to end for next 18 rows = **111 sts**
- Knit one row
- Knit a row of holes (YO K2tog). *This row and the one before and after make the mid-point*
- Knit one row = **111 sts**

KNITTING MARKERS

Knitting markers come in two types: 'place markers' with loops or rings that thread onto needles to mark the place between two stitches, and 'stitch markers' which have hooks and attach to a particular stitch. The pattern requires approximately twenty-four place markers and five stitch markers. Loops of contrasting yarn or thin ribbon, tied into loops, make place markers if necessary. Stitch markers, as the name implies, mark stitches and have a hook which attaches to the stitch.
It is helpful to use different coloured markers at the start of each of the corner sections and a stitch marker for the middle stitch of each corner. This is indicated in the pattern as necessary.

- Knit first 2 sts together then knit to end for next 18 rows = **93 sts**
- Knit a row of holes (YO K2tog)
- Knit first 2 sts together then knit to end for next 18 rows = **75 sts**
- Knit a row of holes (YO K2tog)
- Knit first 2 sts together then knit to end for next 18 rows = **57 sts**
- Knit a row of holes (YO K2tog)
- Knit first 2 sts together then knit to end for next 18 rows = **39 sts**
- Knit a row of holes (YO K2tog)
- Knit first 2 sts together then knit to end for next 18 rows = **21 sts**
- Knit a row of holes (YO K2tog)
- Knit first 2 sts together then knit to end for next 18 rows = **3 sts**

Preparing for the Old Shale section

Structurally, the shawl is built up from this square centre section. Stitches for the wavy Old Shale section are picked up to form six 'waves' down each side. These coincide with holes at every 18th row. The number of stitches down each side (108) remains constant throughout. It is essential to increase the number of stitches as the shawl grows, otherwise it would not lie flat. This is achieved by creating two more waves which radiate out from each corner starting with 3 stitches; it is important to clearly identify the beginning and end of each corner section with a place marker.

- Row 1: in centre colour, with three stitches on the needle and right side facing, place a stitch marker on the first of these stitches which will be recognizable to mark the beginning of the row.
- Before commencing to knit, place a second marker to define the end of the corner section and the beginning of first block of Old Shale pattern down the side.
- Between here and the next row of holes, *pick up and knit 18 stitches, i.e. 1 stitch for every row and place a knitting marker (PM). The Old Shale pattern comprises 18 stitches and coincides with the holes in the centre section. After six blocks of 18 stitches, place corner marker**.
- Pick up and knit three stitches to form the corner section, place marker, and repeat from * to **.
- Row 2: *knit twice into each stitch in the corner section = 6 stitches. Knit a row of holes (YO, K2tog) along next 108 stitches** and repeat from * to ** taking care to keep the markers in place particularly at the corners. A row of holes gives flexibility; holes can enlarge or close up as the need arises and still look good.
- Row 3: purl taking care to maintain the position of the markers, particularly at the corner sections where there are currently 6 stitches.

The spectacular Old Shale – wavy section

Decisions now have to be taken about the sequence of colours for the 'waves' in Old Shale. It can be helpful to simply lay skeins side by side and use the grey-scale technique to see the effect of placing light and dark colours next to each other (*see* Chapter 7). A sequence of ten to twelve 'waves' in different colours works well.

Continue working in rounds, a corner section followed by a side section, as follows. The number of stitches in corner sections increases, while the 108 stitches in each side section remains constant.

Side sections
- Old Shale pattern comprises 4 rows, with new colours introduced on the third row
- Row 1: K1, K2tog (3 times), YO, K1 (5 times) YO, K2tog (3 times) = **18 sts**
- Row 2: knit
- Row 3: change colour and knit from beginning to end
- Row 4: purl from beginning to end

Corner sections
Don't worry if there is a stitch short or over, as long as the overall theme is maintained and the number of stitches is gradually increased towards the goal of 2 × 18 pattern blocks with a consistent marked stitch in the middle radiating out from the corner.

- Corner section 1st pattern row (CS1pr): K1, K1, YO, K1, YO*place stitch marker on this stitch, K1, YO, K2tog, = **8 sts** (*this stitch marks the start of the second block of pattern that makes up the corner section and radiates out from the corner.

- Row 2 knit, Row 3 knit in new colour, Row 4 purl
- CS2pr: K1, K1, YO, K1, YO, K1, K1, K1, YO, K1, YO, K1 = **12 sts**
- Row 2 knit, Row 3 knit in new colour, Row 4 Purl
- CS3pr: K1, K2tog, YO, K1, YO, K1, YO, K1, K1, K1, YO, K1, YO, K1, YO, K1 = **16 sts**
- Row 2 knit, Row 3 knit in new colour, Row 4 purl
- CS4pr: K1, K2tog, YO, K1, YO, K1, YO, K1, YO, K2tog; repeat = **20 (2 × 10) sts**
- Row 2 knit, Row 3 knit in new colour, Row 4 purl
- CS5pr: K1, K2tog, YO, K1, YO, K1, YO, K1, YO, K1, YO, K1, YO, K2tog; repeat = **28 (2 × 14) sts**
- Row 2 knit, Row 3 knit in new colour, Row 4 purl
- CS6pr: K1, K2tog, (K1, YO 7 times), K2tog, K2tog; repeat = **36 (2 × 18) sts**
- Row 2 knit, Row 3 knit in new colour, Row 4 purl

PLAIN SAILING

Now there are two complete wavy sections in each corner the Old Shale 18-stitch pattern repeats all the way round. Simply continue the Old Shale pattern all the way round without interruption at corner sections. It is very pleasing to see the wavy sections develop.

Increase cable length as required and increase needle size about every three Old Shale pattern sections to accommodate the increasing distance around the edge of the shawl.

Continue with Old Shale pattern, changing colours until the colour scheme is completed ending with a colour other than that which will be used for the peaks.

Final phase: the peaks

The peaks are knitted in the same light colour as the central square section which appear again in the Old Shale section as illustrated. Each peak is knitted at right angles to the Old Shale section by casting on 8 new stitches, then knitting back along them and knitting in one stitch (K1tog) from the Old Shale section. Turn and knit back out again – it sounds more complex than it actually is. A stop is placed on the redundant end of the large cable needle and the other needle is re-connected to a short cable. As the last row of the Old Shale section is knitted in a different colour to the peaks it is easy to spot where the last stitch of the peak and first of the Old Shale stitches are knitted together (K1tog) at the end of the incoming row.

With right side facing, remove needle and place a stop on the right-hand cable; fix short cable to the needle and cast on 8 more stitches.

- Turn. Row 1 knit 8, turn
- Row 2 Slip 1, K5, YO, K2 *The pattern starts here.*
- Row 3 YO, K2tog, K6, K2tog, turn
- Row 4 Slip 1, K4, YO, K2tog, YO, K2
- Row 5 YO, K2tog, K7, K2tog, turn
- Row 6 Slip 1, K3, YO, K2tog, YO, K2tog, YO, K2
- Row 7 YO, K2tog, K8, K2tog, turn
- Row 8 Slip 1, K2, YO, K2tog, YO, K2tog, YO, K2tog, YO, K2
- Row 9 YO, K2tog, K9, K2tog, turn
  Point of peak occurs about this area
- Row 10 Slip 1, K2, K2tog, YO, K2tog, YO, K2tog, YO, K2tog, K1
- Row 11 YO, K2tog, K8, K2tog, turn
- Row 12 Slip 1, K3, K2tog, YO, K2tog, YO, K2tog, K1
- Row 13 YO, K2tog, K7, K2tog, turn

'Wisteria' coils art yarn by P. Austin.

- Row 14 Slip 1, K4, K2tog, YO, K2tog, K1
- Row 15 YO, K2tog, K6, K2tog, turn
- Row 16 Slip 1, K5, K2tog, K1
- Row 17 YO, K2tog, K5, K2tog, turn
- Repeat rows 2–17, all the way round
- Cast off and stitch edges of the first and last peaks together

Now it is off the needles, take time to admire it and enjoy this tremendous achievement. But remember, it is still only like a cygnet and has yet to mature into the elegant swan it was designed to be…

Dressing

To dress the shawl, sometimes referred to as blocking or finishing, wash it in warm water carefully without rubbing and rinse in water of the same temperature to avoid risk of felting. Turning such a work of art into felt is a thought too hard to bear! To dry, roll in a towel and squeeze out as much of the excess water as you can.

Either pull out onto a square framework, fixing the point of each peak onto a peg as pictured. Make sure you maintain the overall shape of straight sides with a quadrant of a circle making up each corner. Extra long rubber bands are useful for places where there is not enough stretch. Alternatively, thread a lace through the point of each peak, and stretch out and pin out on a bed mattress or covered carpet. A clean square tablecloth or sheet between the carpet and the shawl will protect both and make it easier to obtain a regular shape during stretching. Leave to dry and set for a few days. The shawl can be redressed as necessary.

And, finally, take pleasure and pride in this hugely satisfying and meaningful work.

THE ART OF YARN

Yarn is a mix of fibre, spinning method, colour, and yarn structure. Art yarn is all of these things, plus something more; its purpose is art. It has a title which usually reflects the meaning; and art yarn bears

'Devastation of the Navajo nation' commemorated in Churro art yarn by J. Heynes.

'Sea Spray' art yarn in mohair incorporates glass beads.

the name of the spinner whose work it is. There is always a catalyst that sparked off its creation. It could be a robin, or the destruction of a nation. There is always something that inspired the spinner to make it.

Sometimes, a fleece will spontaneously inspire a pullover or throw, and that is a lovely thing when it happens, but the result will not be art yarn. Art yarn is not designed, at the outset, to be a knitted woven or crocheted project, although it may end up so one day. Yarn can be simply be yarn, spun with spontaneity and joy, just for the sake of it!

It is easy to define yarn; not so easy to define art. We need to be clear about what we mean by 'art'. It is helpful if one understands art as 'a personal response to something'. Leonardo da Vinci painted the Mona Lisa in 1503; Damien Hurst produced a sheep sculpture in a tank of formaldehyde in 1994. Two totally different concepts, both acknowledged, accepted and, financially, highly valued as art. Their

work is a personal response to something using their chosen medium. Tracey Emin uses her life experiences as well as sculpture, paint, textiles and photography to produce equally acknowledged art. You don't have to be famous to be an artist: in fact very, very few artists are famous, and spinners have little hope of achieving world acclaim either. But it does not stop their artistic expression. Their art is their personal response to something expressed in the medium in which they work. It is just the same for spinners; everyone owns their art. Fame may be highly unlikely, but art yarn can be a certainty if you want to make it.

With art yarn there is always a stimulus, a connection of ideas, or spark of inspiration in the design pathway that triggers it. Paintings by acclaimed artists can be an excellent source of inspiration for art yarn; look at the work of Monet, Matisse, Klimt, for example.

Art yarn it is not necessarily beautiful or pleasing to the eye. No-one would

say that Picasso's *Guernica* is not art. It is his personal response to the devastation of war. It is certainly not beautiful; it is painful and horrid to look at – but still art.

Similarly, Churro fleece is not beautiful, and neither is the story of persecution, deprivation and virtual devastation of the Navajo nation's traditional way of

Sunset rolags and spun yarn changing colours as at sunset.

Sunset spirals art yarn.

life. But it can be art yarn, can tell its own story, and can be seen woven into some serious art by Navajo survivors.

Art yarn is the personal response of a spinner to fibre, texture, colour, structure and technique, and reflects the skill of the person who made it. Art yarn cannot be made 'properly' to a set recipe. It cannot be right or wrong; like a feeling, it is acceptable and belongs to someone. There is no rule book on spinning, nor on art. Purpose differentiates art yarn from any other yarn. Is the reason for its existence art or utility? Yarn that is made to serve a purpose is valued based on whether or not it does what it is intended to do. The purpose could be anything from spinning practice to a utility item, if your preference is to think of it that way.

Any yarn can be beautiful and a source of great joy and pleasure, but that does not make it art yarn. A utility yarn is frequently made in response to the fibre: I have a Herdwick fleece and it will make a good rug. I have this Shetland so will make a shawl. Art yarn is more likely a response to words like, 'I am going to spin this because it reminds me of… / feels like… / is so… / expresses the joy I feel…'.

It is perfectly possible to spin art yarn on a drop spindle or any standard spinning wheel, but both have their limitations. The advantage of the drop spindle is there are no hooks on which fibres can get caught and no orifice to limit the thickness of the singles thread. However, all that twirling and dropping can get a bit tedious, which is why most spinners use a wheel.

Standard spinning wheels have an orifice of only about 1cm diameter which limits the thickness of singles and ply, and loose fibres can easily become tangled on the hooks of flyers. A great wheel has no hooks or orifice, but most homes are not big enough to house them. Many traditional wheels have optional jumbo flyer units with a wider than average orifice and large bobbins. A wheel without an orifice at all, such as Ashford's Joy Freedom Flyer, is an excellent choice for art yarn, as is the Kiwi Superflyer, with its extra wide orifice.

Carders with long, fine pins are essential for mixing fibres, particularly when there is a need to increase light in an art yarn. They also facilitate combining nepps, silk and fine fibre. For fibre, anything goes: comb, shred it, chop it or buy it ready extruded. For colour you can mix, dye and blend – again, anything goes.

For spinning technique, art yarn does not have to stand up to much wear and tear so boundaries can be pushed! It can be as delicate as you like, or rope; you choose.

For interaction with light, there are lustrous silks and long wools, gold and silver thread, Angelina fibre in all colours and textures along with a huge range of commercial cones.

Art yarn is personal. It doesn't have to be beautiful and not everyone that sees it will appreciate it. Your art yarn is your spun response to something that inspires you – something that brings you joy, or satisfaction, or enables expression of life experience or emotion. If others respond agreeably to your art, then that is a bonus. Art is always acceptable to someone at some time or in some place.

IN A NUTSHELL

Yarn comprises fibre, spinning technique, colour and yarn structure. Art yarn comprises all of those things, plus mindfulness and meaning. Like all art, this art yarn is acceptable to someone, and bears a title (source of inspiration) along with the name of the spinner who made it.

Ultimately, all spinning, regardless of its destiny for art or utility, is a question of proficiency, mindfulness and creativity. Like all artists, as spinners become more experienced and skilled their work develops a unique character. It is by pushing the spinning techniques and properties of fibre, colour and structure to the limits, that knowledge, skills and the artistry of spinning has evolved. As we acquire new skills, new fibres and new equipment, then new opportunities and ideas open up all the time. So, say the word, and dream the dream. Get off the treadmill, and make the artistry of yarn happen!

You will not see it written in history books, but at the same time as men and women were painting the walls of caves, they were putting fibre and twist together. Without fibre, they could not have made bows, fixed arrow and axe-heads, transported kill or tied animal skins around themselves to keep warm. Art and spinning is part of our natural being, cave paintings show that it always has been so.

Creating art yarn is as natural as any other artistic thing to do. In fact, you can spin anything you like for art or utility. It is never right or wrong. It is not necessary – or even possible – to obtain a degree in spinning: the skill and artistry of spinning yarn is open to anyone. All that is needed is help and encouragement to set hands to the distaff and get started and follow your own path.

My personal experience is that learning to spin, and creating yarn, is akin to a spiritual journey. In over thirty years of teaching and sharing my enthusiasm for spinning with others, I have witnessed too much healing for it to be an accident. It can bring joy to the heart and solace and support when one does not know how to cope with life. An uplifting, wholesome and affirming craft that transcends the commonplace.

hands to the distaff
will spin
peace in your heart

Rainbow dyed bouclé from dye batch pictured in Chapter 8. Make the artistry happen by choosing the fibre, spinning method, colour, texture, and yarn structure.

Further Reading

Chapter 2

Franquemont, Abby. *Respect the Spindle.* Interweave Press, 2009.

Chapter 3

Anderson, Sarah. *The Spinner's Book of Yarn Designs.* Storey Publishing, 2012.

Chapter 4

Blacker, Sue. *Pure Wool: A Knitter's Guide to Using Single-breed Yarns.* A & C Black, 2012.

Chapter 6

Ross, Mabel. *The Essentials of Yarn Design for Handspinners.* Mabel Ross, 1983.

Chapter 7

Finlay, Victoria. *Colour: Travels Through the Paintbox.* Hodder and Stoughton, 2002.

Menz, Deb. *Color Works.* Interweave Press, 2004.

Menz, Deb. *Color in Spinning.* Interweave Press, 2005.

Chapter 8

Hardman, Judy, and Sally Pinhay. *Natural Dyes.* Crowood Press, 2009.

Milner, Ann. *The Ashford Book of Dyeing.* Ashford Handicrafts Ltd, 2007.

Chapter 9

Varney, Sarah. *Spinning Designer Yarns.* Interweave Press, 2003.

Wild, J.P. *Textile Manufacture in the Northern Roman Provinces.* Cambridge University Press, 2009.

Chapter 10

Miller, Sharon. *Shetland Hap Shawls Then and Now.* Heirloom Knitting, 2006.

Glossary

Andean ply   method making 2-ply yarn from a spindle or bobbin of singles.

Attentuate   process of fibres slipping over each other to form an even yarn.

Britch   coarse fibres of fleece from around the back leg area of sheep.

Carders   hand-held wooden boards with pins for preparing fleece for spinning.

Carding   preparing wool for spinning with carders.

Core spinning   wrapping fibre around a previously made core.

Crimp   natural waves or crinkles in fleece fibre.

Doubling   traditional term for plying 2-ply.

Drafting   letting of fibres, prior to twist being allowed in, in the spinning process.

Drawing   stretching out fibre and twist together in the spinning process.

Flyer   part of the spinning wheel that puts twist into thread and winds spun thread onto the bobbin.

Footman   part of the spinning wheel that connects the footplate to the crank of the axle.

Heddle   hole through which a warp thread passes

In the grease   unwashed fleece as it came off the sheep.

Kemp   coarse fibres released into fleece for extra protection.

Lazy Kate   device to hold bobbins when plying.

Leader thread   thread attached to a bobbin or spindle onto which new fibres are spun.

Lock   natural growth of small clusters of fibre in fleece.

Long draw   creating an arm's length of woollen thread in one movement.

Lustre   natural sheen commonly seen in long wool fleece.

Maidens   part of spinning wheel that supports the flyer.

Micron   1/1000 millimetre, used for measuring fibre thickness.

Mordant   chemical used to pre-condition fibres prior to dyeing

Mother-of-all   part of the spinning wheel that supports maidens.

Navajo ply   method of creating 3-ply yarn from a single bobbin.

Nepps   tiny particles of felted woollen fibres

Niddy-Noddy   device for making skeins.

Orifice   part of the spinning wheel flyer through which the leader thread passes.

Plying   twisting two or more singles threads together in the opposite direction to spinning in order to create stable yarn.

Raddle   residual coloured wax found in fleece from crayon used to mark sheep.

Rolag   carded fleece prepared in cylindrical formation for hand spinning.

Roving   carded fibres lying lengthways in a long cylindrical formation. Can refer to either high-volume commercially processed fibre, or short, fine, hand-processed lengths.

Sett   proximity of warp threads, usually measured in threads per inch

Shearling   a sheep that is due for its first shearing at about one year old.

Singles   thread which has been spun, but not plied.

Skirting   removal of britch, belly and coarse wool at the extremities of a shorn fleece.

Squirmal   a short section of singles thread that has doubled back on itself.

Staple   cluster of fleece fibre measured from cut end to tip.

Warp   long threads attached to the loom in weaving.

Weft   threads woven between warps from a shuttle in weaving.

Woollen   thread spun from fibres lying across the leader thread.

Worsted   thread spun from fibres lying parallel to the leader thread.

Wraps per inch   method of measuring the thickness of spun yarn by wrapping it around a ruler.

Index